BURY ME IN MY BOOTS

BURY ME
IN MY BOOTS

by

SALLY TRENCH

HODDER AND STOUGHTON

LONDON SYDNEY AUCKLAND TORONTO

AUTHOR'S PREFACE TO THE PAPERBACK EDITION

Two years have elapsed since I completed this true and somewhat frightening story of how many thousands of us manage to exist from day to day, alone, rootless, without hope. Since then I have lost my anonymity in the sub-world of Skid Row and instead have become an A.A. (Accidental Author), a wife and instant Mum to six step-children and a mother in my own right. Yet my identity with the neglected and uncared for thankfully remains, and if I can impart a little of those early experiences to others in my secure every-day life now, I will not have failed God or my family or those I shared so much with and loved so dearly.

June, 1969   SALLY TRENCH

FOREWORD

SALLY TRENCH blew into my life in this way.

Last year, some nuns I knew spoke to me about her in glowing terms. They had expelled her from school some five years earlier when she was about sixteen, but it was a case of the ugly duckling for now she was doing wonderful work among the down-and-outs. However, they were anxious about the state of her soul. With all this good work she was doing, was she still keeping close to God?

At that time I was editing a little magazine, so I wrote to Sally asking for an article. She sent me one, and I sent her a cheque and asked her to come round to discuss one or two points in what she had written.

This was sheer jesuitry, of course, but it worked and she came along and we got acquainted and I was able to set the nuns' minds at rest.

But Sally seemed almost too good to be true, and although I believed her story I wanted to see for myself. So one evening last January we set out together to look up some of her friends.

We drove over London Bridge, turned north-east and, after passing through some narrow streets, found ourselves alongside an acre of derelict land, the sit of bomb damage twenty-five years ago.

With torches in our hands we made our way across mud and the débris of bricks and concrete to a group of nine or ten men sitting round a fire.

When they saw Sally they stood up and shouted greetings. As we came up, she introduced me, "A friend I've brought along." I shook hands with the men on my side of the fire. They called me 'Father' or 'Reverend'.

We stayed there about half an hour. Sally laughed and talked with them all, handing round cigarettes and asking if anyone had any cuts or wounds she could attend to. One man had fallen into the fire while drunk and his hands were badly burned. She treated them and bandaged them up.

Meanwhile, sitting on a rusty petrol drum, I talked with those near me.

There was Henry, who seemed very drunk and kept asking me about the patron saint of thieves. He came from the Shetland Isles. Sally was pleased with his condition because he was drunk on surgical spirits, which was better than being drunk on meths.

Then there was a man from Longford who never smiled or joked and kept telling me of what clothes he needed. He fought shy of talking about Longford.

Jock came from Aberdeen and reproached Sally for not having brought him the trousers she had promised him. She said that she had not promised to bring them *that* night, but that she would soon.

Then there was Pat who talked nostalgically about Dublin. He was very friendly and more than half drunk. He soon disappeared to go begging.

When we got up to go, they made me promise that I'd be back soon. It was all most pathetic, although I had seen them at their best: it was a warm, fine night, the ground was not too wet, and they were all relatively sober. A week or so before, some boys had burst in on them and beaten them up. So Sally had found them another site with a camouflaged entrance, where they went for sleeping. We went there now.

It was another open bombed site, even worse than the first, with great chunks of masonry lying around. Sally told me to beware of rats, as she had twice been bitten there and had had to get some anti-tetanus treatment in hospital. As we threaded our way through the débris, she pointed to a corner of the site and said, "I found a man dead there one day."

She had covered the entrance to this site with a moveable piece of corrugated iron, and another piece concealed the entrance to a fragment of a house that was still standing.

8

She was very proud of this as she had fixed the roof (or what was left of it) herself. We looked in the one room there was: we saw a litter of bits and pieces of sacking and filthy blanket, with bottles and broken glass here and there. And the smell!

To see our next hide-out, we had to crawl on hands and knees through openings about two feet high; perhaps it had been an air-raid shelter of sorts. Again there was the litter of sacking and rags, and always the bottles, broken and unbroken.

Our next call was at a three-storey derelict house. Like the two previous places, this one was empty. The occupants (and Sally told me there would be thirty people sleeping there) were out procuring their meths or whatever was their addiction. Again, there was all the filth, the rags, the bottles, the smell.

Sally told me that there were more than a hundred such places she could take me to, but I was already beginning to feel that I'd had enough. So we went to just one more place.

It was a derelict cellar, quite the ultimate in squalor. Here we found an old man with an ulcerous foot. He was already on Sally's 'panel', and she dressed the wound for him. We chatted for a while and then bade him good night and left. (The pathos of that 'good night'! It nearly made one weep. How many years would it have been since he had known a good night?)

Sally then drove me home. I gave her a pair of trousers for Jock and some other clothes, and while I went off to bed she set out on her nightly round.

Sally's is an unusual apostolate—unusual, perhaps, because most of us are too calculating and uncommited in the living of our faith.

Her apostolate is unusual, but it is authentically Christian. Her books shows this. Many people will say that it can't be true. But it is. She is no twentieth-century beatnik playing the compassion game. She is a Christian, in love with Christ

9

and with her fellowmen. And her apostolate to them has a long tradition. How many of the saints have seen and helped Christ in the poor and under-privileged! St. Francis of Assisi, St. Elizabeth of Hungary, St. Vincent de Paul! Sally too has caught sight of what they saw.

And while we pray that God may look after her and keep her humble and go on using her to help His poor, we can also pray for ourselves: that we too may see Him in the socially inadequate—that we may see Him and have the courage to help Him.

Hugh S. Thwaites, S.J.
4th September, 1967

S. George's,
Sansome Place,
Worcester.

CHAPTER ONE

It was surrounded by a high wall and barbed wire. There was one entrance and one exit. The grounds were well kept and the many match-box buildings were of a clinical appearance. It looked like a prison; and in its corridors, behind those formidable walls, I could feel the sense of foreboding that hangs round our penal institutions. When I was told where I was, I felt as if I had been kicked in the stomach. I was in a mental hospital.

I lay in my bed stunned by the news, all sorts of imaginative thoughts flashing across my mind.

"Why couldn't you walk when the ambulance men brought you in?" The staff nurse was standing over me writing down a list of all the gear I had brought in.

"I don't know," I feebly replied, and as an afterthought, "I suppose because I'm so tired." I had forgotten that I had been carried in.

"Right, I've emptied your haversack and I think I've got all the items down. I've taken your money and your passport to put in the office. Will you sign here?" I could have been signing my death warrant for all I cared. God, I felt tired.

The staff nurse was talking again: "I'll bring you a cup of hot chocolate and then you can sleep. The doctor will be seeing you in the morning."

"Go to hell," I thought, "just leave me alone." She did, but not for long.

"Here you are, drink this up, it'll do you good." Obediently I drank it. "Sleep well." She seemed to drift from sight. Dear God, I was tired.

It was morning, and the daily bustle of the ward penetrated my sleep. I did not want to open my eyes. I had no wish to face reality, the stigma of my surroundings, the endless day ahead .

"Hello, you awake?" a pimply face bent over me. "Got a fag" she continued. "I'm Christine. Got a fag?" I shook my head. She wrapped her dressing gown around her and walked away, obviously uninterested now that she had learnt I had not brought any cigarettes in with me. I glanced at my watch. It was only 7.30 a.m. I groaned and buried my face in the pillow. How I ached, as if every limb had been torn from me, and my head felt like a lump of lead.

"Everyone up. Mrs. Forbes, your turn to do the floor. Doris, get up and go and wash; get out of that bed at once." It reminded me of my old boarding school. "You must be Sally Trench. You can stay in bed." The sister moved on to the next bed. "Time to get up, Nula." She shook the dormant body beside me. "Nurse, will you see that Mrs. Forbes washes herself?" Patients and nurses scuttled past and only Sister's voice was to be heard. I dozed fitfully.

"Wake up, Miss Trench, here's your breakfast. Shall I put your pillows up for you?" I raised myself on to my elbows and tried to sit up; only then did I realise how weak I was. The nurse helped. "There you are, dear. Eat that up and you'll feel better." She smiled kindly and patted my shoulder reassuringly. I ate my porridge slowly, assimilating my present environment. I was in a ward with thirty empty beds; no, the one at the far end was not empty for I could see a bulge under the blankets. A nurse in a blue pin-stripe uniform came through the door.

"Where is everyone?" I asked.

"Having breakfast in the refectory."

Well at least we're allowed up, I thought. What did it matter anyway? I lay back exhausted. Someone entered. I shut my eyes and feigned sleep. Thoughts on the past year flooded back to me: the fighting of the past six weeks to keep the cause alive; the desperation of the last two weeks and my own sudden collapse twenty-four hours ago. I heard weeping—or did I? Yes, coming from my left. I hauled myself into a sitting position. "Can I help?"

A young girl looked up, not much older than myself I would have thought, with straight black hair draping over her red cardigan. Tears were spilling down her clear pale face. "No, it's nothing."

I smiled. "I always say that but it's never true."

"It's the sister, she has it in for me; if it's not one thing, it's another." Again she wept into her handkerchief.

"Come over here and talk to me. I feel just as miserable as you, you know. No one's spoken to me yet apart from the staff." She came and sat on my bed. "My name's Sally. I was brought in last night."

"I know. I'm Nula. I've been here two weeks."

I felt a little lost for conversation, for I did not want to be tactless enough to ask her what she was here for. "What's this place like—a mad house?"

"No, and don't let anyone tell you it is," she burst out. "They might be mad over in the main buildings, but not in here."

"Well, I'm not mad; a crazy mixed-up kid perhaps, but not mad."

"What happened to you to get you in here, then?"

"Collapse from overwork and exhaustion basically. I think they call it a nervous breakdown."

"That all? That's nothing. You should see some of the cranks here. Some of them have been here years. At least they don't lock you up in this ward, you're free to come and go within reason."

"What! no padded cells?" I joked, and regretted it instantaneously.

"There, over the other side with the lock-up wards." I fell silent.

"What's your work anyway, or are you still at school?"

"Social worker," I replied, and quickly changed the subject. "Will I be allowed up or will I be kept in bed?"

"Oh, they'll let you up when they're ready, or they might keep you under sedation if you're violent. Or they might do what they did to Dot, give you deep sleep treatment. It depends how bad you are."

"Nothing wrong with me that sleep won't cure." I tried to sound convincing. We were interrupted by a nurse calling

13

Nula for her medicine. "See you later," she called quite cheerfully as she left.

Well, I'd helped her forget her tears, but she had left me in a state of apprehension. Patients seemed to drift in and out throughout the morning; females of all description, fat, thin, old and young, each one with a haunted look, each one with her own problem. Some of the more pathetic figures rested on their beds, whilst others just wandered up the ward staring vacantly into the distance and then back again. Christine padded over to me. I noticed she had a cigarette hanging from the corner of her lips.

"Hello, won't they allow you up either? They've kept me in bed for the past four days. It's not my fault. You see, I told my doctor I was going to do away with myself and he's just waiting for me to do it now."

"Nonsense! You're letting your imagination run away with you. He just wants you to get well. How long have you been here?"

"About a year now." I tried to hide my horror. "I don't mind really, it's just my little girl, you know what it is? You see I'm sick up top." She pointed to her head and continued, "If only I hadn't told my doctor. He's waiting for me to do it now."

I was glad that we were interrupted by the doctor. "Go back to bed, Christine." She obeyed meekly. "Miss Trench?" He peered at me through thick-rimmed spectacles, and gave me a quick bow. He was an Indian of very slight build, with a pleasant face. In silence he began to examine me. "There's nothing really wrong with me," I assured him.

He straightened himself and politely replied, "If there wasn't anything wrong with you, Miss Trench, you wouldn't be here and nor would I." I decided not to say another word.

Having scratched my toes, peered into my mouth and pressed my tummy, he seemed fairly satisfied. "You stay in bed today and sleep. Tomorrow you get up and we will talk." How ghastly I thought.

"Talk about what?"

"Your troubles, your work and why you are here." I groaned inwardly.

"I haven't any troubles now; they're all over ... and ... so is my work."

"We will talk." Another quick bow and he was gone. So I was going to have a talk to him? Like hell I was. As if he could understand. I felt very lonely, as if I had been torn naked from the world. I had. My world had been smashed yesterday when everything I had believed in, worked for and fought for had collapsed under the hand of a misguided idealist.

"Hi, you look miserable. It's no good thinking in here." It was Nula.

"Just meditating. The doctor said I've got to stay in bed today and have a talk with him tomorrow."

"That's the usual procedure. You're all right, you've nothing to hide." I glanced at her questioningly. "You're not a potential suicide like me." Proudly she waved her wrists in front of me. "Sixteen stitches in one, and eighteen in the other."

I stared at the two slashes cruelly red against her lily-white skin. "With a razor," she confirmed. "Second time I've tried, but luck hasn't been on my side." How brazen she was.

I spoke quietly, "Nula, don't ever try it again; truly it's not a way out."

"I won't be able to as long as they keep me here. Anyway, what do you care? You can't understand. You don't know what it's like to have a couple of kids and nowhere to sleep them, let alone who their fathers are. Christ, the times I've sat up all night wondering where the next slice of bread's going to come from and whether I'm going to have to sell myself to another man tomorrow night. Kid, you haven't met life yet." She spoke with bitterness and hatred.

"Nula, I may not have suffered your experiences, but I have seen life. I know the smell of the unwanted homeless, and the neglected and helpless. Before now I have sat with dirty and drunk men, infested with bugs, who are dying, in order to hold their hands so that they might realise there is

15

someone in this world who cares whether they live or die. I've held down junkies when they've been frantic for a fix and I've held up alcholics whilst they've vomited into the gutter. I do know the digust and horror of losing one's self-respect and I also know hiding from it is not the answer." She was staring at me, incredulous. I shrugged my shoulders and wished I had not said anything. "Forget it—just remember, running from yourself won't solve your problems." I yawned and closed my eyes. "I'm going to catch up on some of that much needed sleep; see you later." She took the hint and left.

Next morning I roused myself with the rest of the patients. I was entering the wash-room when I heard a scream. "Don't touch me, don't touch me!" In the corner, clinging to the wall in apparent fear of her life, was a middle-aged woman with short-cropped grey hair. Grinning at her nearby was a young coloured girl. "Don't touch me, don't touch me!" the screams continued.

"Shut up, Olive," came a voice from behind one of the shower curtains.

A nurse arrived. "Now, dear, no one is going to touch you. Go back to the ward." Olive pressed herself further against the wall. "I can't while she's standing there; I'll touch her." The nurse led me aside, and the intimidated Olive shrank by. I noticed through my mirror that the girl opposite was furtively watching me. I could not understand why until she took the towel from round her neck. Two ugly rope marks indented her skin. Another potential suicide!

I had breakfast on Nula's table and then lined up with the other patients for my medicine. "Come and join us after in the sitting-room?" Nula called. A few minutes later I was being introduced to Dot and Rita.

"What's the date today?" No one seemed to know.

"Anyone heard the news?" No one had.

"Well, whose turn is it today for a chin-wag with the doctor?" No one knew and no one really cared. They puffed away at their cigarettes.

"Can you go out if you want to?" I broke the silence.

"If you have the doc's permission."

"What do you do all day?"

"Nothing."

"Is there any organised group therapy?"

"Yes." This was hard work, but I persevered.

"When's lunch?" It was an incongruous question, having only just finished breakfast. No one seemed inclined to answer. The coloured girl came up behind Dot and extended her hand for a cigarette. "Don't touch me, don't touch me," Dot shouted jokingly. Everyone laughed. I looked round the room and saw Olive sitting alone tearfully watching Dot's act.

"Lay off, Dot." Nula said it for me and rose to wander over to talk kindly to Olive. Suddenly, for the first time since I had arrived, I could have wept. Here, shut away from the rest of the world were people, all worthwhile and in their own way with something to offer, yet unable to play their part because they could not face or overcome their problem. What a waste!

"Miss Trench, the doctor will see you in room 12," a nurse called. My heart leapt into mouth. "Good luck," someone called. "It's down the corridor on the left."

"Come in." The doctor relaxed in an armchair behind a desk. "Sit down. I hope you slept well last night?"

"Yes thanks."

"Now tell me all about yourself."

"Where do you want me to start?"

"At the beginning."

"Er ... yes, of course. I was born in Woking ... you want me to go back that far?"

"Yes, yes, that's the beginning isn't it?" I grunted. In for a penny, in for a pound! I gave him my life history, at least as much of it as I was prepared to give him, with some additional fabrications put in here and there for good measure. "And that's it so far," I concluded. I wondered how perceptive he was.

"Mmm!" he sat twiddling his pencil, watching me. "And what do you intend to do when you leave here?"

"Who knows? When can I leave?"

"When you like—you're a voluntary patient. I advise you to stay a week and rest, but you can discharge yourself whenever you wish." This piece of news brightened me no end. "Meanwhile I should think about your future and put the past behind you. I can put you in touch with our social worker if you like, she might be able to help you."

"No thanks, I can stand on my own two feet. I'll see you around then."

I closed the door behind me. So I was free to go when I liked. What a difference it made to my outlook! I made my way back to the sitting-room, and as I passed the sister's office, I saw a thin lady carrying two cases talking to the nurse. "Sister said I'd never cope. She was right. I've come back." I heard the nurse's reply also: "Well, we thought you would, dear, so we kept your bed vacant."

For five days more I stayed as a voluntary patient, observing, listening and helping. The time came when I knew that I was fit enough to leave, so I collected my haversack and belongings and said my farewells and stepped once again into the world. What the future held, I did not know, but I cared as I had never cared before. The past year's experience had given me a wealth of knowledge and understanding of human nature, but the past week in hospital had managed to give me more than I could have ever asked for. Now the time had come to start again and use this wealth. No longer was I a naïve do-gooder, a kid with a big heart, but a real person with a job to do. How very different from eighteen months ago when I, as a rebellious teenager, decided to make my stamp on the world. Wrapped in my own self-importance, I thought it was in my power to help everyone less fortunate than myself. I learnt from my mistakes the hard way!

CHAPTER TWO

I HAD always been a presumptuous child. I was the sort of ghastly kid that everyone dreaded having, the kind that if you said, "Don't speak to strange men", would go in search of strangers to talk to, and the more weird and strange they were the better. A proper St. Trinian's pupil!

My interest in the 'social inadequate' developed from my hero-worshipping of tramps. How I envied their way of life, so free and wild, a world of their own. I loved to listen to their tales as much as I loved to tell my own, truth or fiction! When I left boarding school I went in search of a lost cause, determined to play a role in society. I found it on Waterloo Station.

I was coming home very late one night from the country, feeling weary and looking forward to a warm bed. Against a background noise of chamber music intermingled with the groans and sneezings of the engines, I passed the ticket office into the main hall. "Oh, I beg your pardon!" I swung round to see who I had bumped into. She was an old lady, so wrapped up in moth-eaten scarves that her face was hardly visible. She wore a dress down to her ankles and a man's sweater, three times too big for her. She had no stockings, but a pair of disintegrating slippers covered part of her feet. She stood hunched over her brown paper parcels; I do not think she had noticed the impact as I had collided with her, not to mention my apology. I walked on. I noticed scruffy men bedded down under newspapers on the benches, others slouched dejectedly in the corners. They were all dirty and unshaven, a few of the lucky ones had overcoats to protect them against the winter nights, the rest just sat shivering. How easy it was to walk past. How easy it was to sympathise from a distance. How easy it was to pass by on the other side of the road like the Levite in the New Testament.

I stopped and turned back. I parked myself in the middle of a bench between two of the scruffiest men. All at once my Good Samaritan intentions left me and I became nervous. The men had not batted an eyelid. I could smell the alcohol. I fumbled in my pockets for cigarettes and, as I lit one, the two men seemed to wake up. One lurched sideways and leaned against me. I was really frightened. "Go' any to spare?" he slurred. I lit one and handed it to him and repeated the gesture for the bloke on my other side. The man was becoming heavy. If I edged away he might take offence, so I did the only thing possible. I took him by the shoulders and straightened him.

"Want any help, Missy?" A large West Indian, with his hands on his hips, a hat pushed to one side, and a most amiable grin on his round face, swayed before me. "You don't belong here, Missy, not a high-class filly like you," he reprimanded gently.

"I'm not a permanent, just passing through," I said hastily.

"Just visiting You're too pretty to be amongst us dirty drunks. You're not one of us. Go home."

"I will. I just thought they might like a cigarette. What will happen to them? Will they go home?" He threw back his head and laughed.

"Home? Man they got no home. This is their bedroom for tonight." He bent down to me. "Now you go home yourself, Missy, and don't you worry about us. Go home and thank the good Lord you got a home to go to."

The background music had stopped, the engines were bedded down and the station porters were calling out their final farewells. The vast station, an active terminus during the day, was silent save for the periodical cooing of a sleepless pigeon. The homeless, neglected and unwanted shivered under their newspapers. I shoved the packet of cigarettes into the West Indian's hands and did as I was told. I left the cold and hungry dossers to the night. But when I lay in my warm bed with my dog at my feet and a glass of hot chocolate in my hand, I did thank the kind Lord for having blessed me with a family and a home.

The following morning I was exercising my Afghan hound in the park when I came across a similar character to those of the previous night. He was prodding around in the litter bins in search of scraps. I smiled at him as I passed, and said "Good morning". He gave an inaudible grunt, picked up a dog-end and shuffled off in the opposite direction. I wondered where he had spent the night.

Just after midnight I dressed quickly in my jeans and placed the Thermos flask of coffee that I had made that evening in my haversack. The dog wagged his tail with excitement. "Not this time," I whispered, "And don't you dare bark when I come back." I patted him. Despondently, he jumped back on to my bed and watched me open the window and climb out on the window-sill. I wished that our stairs did not creak and that my father was not such a light sleeper. But he was, and the stairs did creak abominably, so there was only the drain-pipe left. By the time I had reached the bottom and climbed down the wall, I was a nervous wreck. A car had passed with its headlights on, and a courting couple had inconveniently halted under the tree where I had intended to descend, so I had been forced to deviate from the route I had worked out in daylight. Trembling, I opened the garage and felt for my bicycle. It was as I had left it. I closed the door gently behind me and crossed to the other side of the road and waited. I expected the lights to come on in the house as father discovered his beloved daughter was not in bed. A full ten minutes I waited. I was in the clear, no one had heard me. Relieved, I bicycled over to Waterloo Station.

It was as cold and silent as the other night. Underneath the newspapers were the same grey debauched faces. I lowered my haversack and poured out the coffee. Someone had woken up, another was stirring. I handed them the hot cups. Along the line of benches, the bodies shifted and haggard faces appeared. I refilled the cups and passed them down the line. I placed cigarettes between icy-mauve lips and poured out more hot coffee for grabbing hands. When I ran dry, I went over to the hot drinks machine and bought more and rationed it to half a cup per man. Cigarettes were being divided also.

The big clock struck two, and as it did so a general move took place. Dossers staggered to their feet, their eyes still closed, and wandered off; they were still asleep as they walked into the telephone booths or down the station where they could not be seen. Some, on hearing the move, automatically rolled off the benches, still snoring, picked themselves up and sauntered behind closed bookstalls where they stood up asleep, hanging on to the bars or the grill. At first I was nonplussed, but I soon discovered the reason for it. In the distance I saw the blue uniforms. Quickly I collected up my pieces and hid myself in the shadows of the arches. I had a front-stall view! There were two of them, and between them they woke every man up. They were polite until the man proved obstreperous or difficult, then they just hauled him to his feet and shoved him towards the exit. Some they escorted off the premises, others they dragged away roughly. The more respectable-looking citizens they asked to see their tickets, for there were a few who were staying the night to catch the first trains at dawn. If they failed to produce a ticket, they were removed too. I was to learn later that this was a regular two-hourly feature throughout the night. Part of the routine for the law-boys, but a purely symbolic gesture, for they later stood by and watched the same faces reappear and did not bother to move them on till two hours later. I retreated to my bike, passing sleeping men still on their feet, but the general drift back to the benches had begun.

My routine with the dossers on Waterloo Station became a regular shift. I learnt to sleep till two, be at the station by three and home by four. Even my nerves were becoming nerveless! The drain-pipe climb was a piece of cake! The lads at the station became as accustomed to the whiff of hot coffee in their sleep, as they did to the two-hourly move-on.

Only once my luck ran out. I was perched on the window-sill adjusting my haversack before commencing my now fairly agile descent. There was quite a wind blowing, and the trees were whispering in chorus beneath a quarter-moon. My eyes were accustomed to the dark shapes around me and my ears always alert for unfamiliar sounds. Down the drain-pipe on to the terrace, a few steps and over a ledge, along the garage roof and over the wall. I jumped on to the pavement. I saw little and heard less. I rubbed my grubby hands and took off my gym shoes in the shadow of the garage.

"Quite a circus act, that!" Out of the same shadows loomed a policeman. "Well, any more tricks tonight?"

I tried to appear calm and dignified. "Hello, officer. You must have thought that a bit odd?"

He drew himself up to his full height, "To say the least."

"Oh, please. Don't think the worst. I do it regularly." Somehow that did not sound the right thing to say.

"I'm sure you do. A different house each time, no doubt?"

"Oh, no. Never. I do live there, you know.'

"You live there," he affirmed agreeably. "And because there are no doors to your house, unlike every other house, you have a drainpipe. Right?"

"I didn't want to wake my parents and our stairs creak." It all sounded most unconvincing.

"Any way of identifying yourself?"

I dug into my pockets and went through my haversack and produced a filthy handkerchief and a purse.

"What's all this?" He had tipped my ten packets of cigarettes out followed by the bottles and flasks of coffee. "Not thinking of coming home for a while, or are you just a chain smoker?"

I recited the narrative of my night vigils at the station.

"It all sounds very good and Christian, if it's true, though highly improper for a young girl like you. And how do you get to the other side of the Embankment at this time of night?" Of course, how stupid of me, that was proof in itself. I produced the garage key from my purse and showed him my bike. "How's that for evidence?" We parted the best of friends, and on many occasions after that meeting I used to wave to him from my drain-pipe as he walked his beat. I also arranged with him that he should pass the word around to his colleagues should he be taken off night duty. I never again had police trouble and was often greeted by some strange policeman who addressed me by my Christian name. My friends and neighbours were often to raise an eyebrow at this!

I found my time was so scarce, not to mention busy, during my hour at the station, that I never managed to get to know the characters and the stories behind them till some months later. The most pathetic case I discovered was Jane, the lady I collided with that first night. For ten years, Jane had been dividing her time between Victoria and Waterloo Stations. During the day she hung around the platforms and pigeons at Victoria until it closed down at night, when she would drift over to Waterloo to pass the long nights. She possessed nothing but her brown paper parcels which contained anything she could beg or pick out of litter bins, and the worn thin clothes she stood up in. Another was Bulldog, so named because of his squashed-in features and flabby jowls. He suffered from what is now commonly termed 'war neurosis', but what is better known as shell-shock. He had periodic hallucinations and thought the Germans were after him and every time an engine in the station blew steam, he used to dive under a bench under the impression that it was a grenade exploding. Then there was Baldy, for whom I had a very soft spot. Baldy joined the school of drunks and dossers on the station because he refused to live in any of the large hostels with all their rules and regulations. He was a little man whom the wind could have blown away any time, but he was tough and hardy despite his looks, and the most even-tempered man I have ever met. He was seventy-four and had served in both world wars. There was very little Baldy had not done in his life, and he had become wise with his experiences. How wasted he was, living as a dosser whom no one noticed as they charged by to catch their après-work trains to take them home to a family, a warm house and a cooked meal. But after all, these people had become part of the scenery, they were there every night without fail. Fragile, sick, with no one to care for them, least of all love them. It was easy not to notice them. Some had been kipping out in the cold for years, others had just come down to London to try their luck in the Great Metropolis and had no money and nowhere to stay, so the station became their bedroom too.

Over the months I came to realise that social inadequacy was a problem that was becoming more and more pressing: the number of down-and-outs seemed to be increasing, even in this day of the Welfare State. There were a mere handful who were professionally concerned with their care, and there were others, admittedly, whose occupations were unconnected with the problem and who interested themselves on a part-time basis. But it was all too clear that there were too few prepared to assist them. Perhaps it was fear that held them back. Indeed these were people we would prefer not to know, drifters, dossers, down-and-outs, call them what you will. But I could not escape from the fact that they were homeless and rootless, unwanted and very much alone. They were too afraid of the organised social services, and too nervous to live long in the big hostels with all the regimentations and quarrels found there, so they drifted on to Waterloo Station, or in and out of prison and hospital, just to find a bed. They were the rejects with nothing to live for. They were the people who could not, or would not, by helped by the Welfare State, because they were unable to face the demands, pressures and responsibilities of our society. One did not know them, often one did not even see them, but they were there, waiting for death to relieve them of their living hell.

I began to realise that my coffee trips were futile—they only brought temporary relief whereas these people needed something more permanent with more individual care and attention. But the needs of these outcasts were insufficiently met or even understood by the public. To give them practical help needed money, time and professional skills. Of which I had none. My own inadequacy to assist them haunted me, so I went in search of others who felt the same. I found people kind and sympathetic, but not prepared to stick their necks out and become involved. What was so frustrating, most of the objections they offered were reasonable. After all, the down-and-out was an unattractive figure. He was pitiful and, at the same time, inspired a sense of disgust and exasperation in any self-respecting person, that he could drift so far from any contact with responsibility. Was an unhappy childhood, a broken home, war neurosis, or any other commonly cited cause enough to bring a man to that point of degradation? Who were we to judge? Whatever the cause, I felt it was society's responsibility to help break their pattern since they did rely on us as their fellow-men. Thus I was determined to reinstate the rejected from their no-man's-land, not on a temporary basis but permanently. How I was intending to do this I had no idea, and after a short space of time I realised that it would not be with the support of my family or friends who so strongly disapproved.

CHAPTER THREE

IT was by the hand of fate that I was walking up Ladbroke Grove, an indigent area of London, one evening when I came across a down-and-out sprawled in the gutter. He was groaning quietly as if in pain. People just walked past as if they had not seen him. I knelt down beside him and turned him on to his back. I could not see his face for dirt. "What's the trouble?"

"They hit me."

"Who?"

"Them blokes." I could see no one apart from the occasional passer-by.

"Where do you live?"

"Golborne."

"Where's that?"

"Up that road there."

"Do you think you can stand? Have a bash and I'll help you back."

Together we stumbled to our feet, hanging on to each other, and with his arm round my neck we began to walk leisurely back—to Golborne. Crammed tightly in the middle of a row of shops, just off the Portobello Road, behind a vegetable and fruit stall, was the Golborne Centre. We pushed open the unlatched front door and walked in. I was staggered, we were standing in a church. It was a large drab room with a pulpit at one end looking down on rows of shabby chairs and cigarette ends and up at a false roof stretching across to hide what was once a circular gallery. My companion led me to the spiral staircase. It was an ancient one, of wrought iron, just wide enough for one man to ascend at a time. We climbed into the gallery. It was packed with two-tier bunks and narrow steel lockers. I clung to a bunk looking down at the false roof which, though safe enough, had a precarious feel to it. I helped the old man on to his bed and he lay there huddled in equally old blankets. I descended the spiral staircase even more gingerly than I had climbed it and went in search of someone.

I found a tiny kitchen with two old gas stoves in it but no people. It was partitioned off from the church, and from it I could hear talking in the next partitioned room. As I entered, the smell of tobacco was overpowering and visibility very poor. I was in a fair-sized room, filthy and bleak, but warm. Crippled tables and chairs stood around on which were hunched vagrants, delinquents, ex-convicts and inadequates. A battered television set at the other end was the only other piece of furniture. No one looked up as I made my way through dog-ends and dinner scraps on the bare wooden floor. I sat myself beside a young man with shoulder-length hair. His features were sharp and his eyes cold and narrow; a dangerous friend to make, I thought.

"Hello. Like a cigarette?" I gave him a friendly smile. His eyes narrowed to almost closing; from his pocket he pulled some loose tobacco and began to roll his own. I put mine away. He watched me suspiciously.

"I brought back one of your chaps," I explained. He continued rolling his cigarette, watching me like a hawk.

"I took him upstairs to his bunk." Pause. "I hope that's all right?" He put the cigarette between his lips and slowly went through his pockets, never taking his eyes off me. He produced a lighter and flicked it alight. Instead of lighting his cigarette, he enlarged the flame. I felt his shifty eyes burning behind that flame. I sat, cold with fear, wondering what his next move was going to be. Suddenly he stuck the lighter under my nose. I threw my head back to avoid the heat, and with clenched fists banged his arm on to the table. It was an automatic reaction. Fear gripped me for his face was red with rage. He spat the cigarette out and rolled his eyes and laughed. "You're not f . . . bad," he commented.

"Thank you," I said dryly, not sharing the joke. "You're not bad at making friends yourself." I found myself saying this angrily before I could check myself. He glanced at me and burst into more laughter.

"You should have seen your face; right green you were."

"Now that we're talking, who's in charge here?" I enquired.

"Depends 'ow you look on it, don't it? No one's in charge of me."

"Well, who runs the place then?"

"The Guv'." Patience was never my virtue.

"And who's the Guv'?"

"Peake, the Right Reverend Peake."

"Where would I find him?"

"Gone 'ome."

"Well, who's in charge while he's away?" He grinned at me and I noticed his front teeth were missing.

"Dunno."

The door swung open and a tall grey-bearded man entered. He saw me and came over. "Can I help you?"

"Well, actually I just brought back one of your lads, I found him in Ladbroke Grove. Apparently, there was a fight."

"That was good of you. Thanks. Would you like to come into the office?" I rose to follow him.

"Thank you for nothin'. Good-bye." The young man I had been talking to threw back his chair and pushed in front of me and out of the door in a temper. Greybeard turned to me: "Don't take any notice of Bob, he's got a temperature like a yo-yo!"

In the office I learned from Dave (he told me his name later) that the Reverend Peake, a Nonconformist minister, had turned his church into a doss-house some years previously, and could now sleep anything up to fifty men. He offered them the draughty protection of his church and three square meals a day; it was not a lot, but a castle compared with the Embankment or the gutter. At first the minister slept them in the gallery among the pews, and they used to hang their washing across the church and over the pulpit; by their very presence, three-quarters of his congregation, who considered that this was carrying practical Christianity to unreasonable lengths, refused to come to his services. But the project grew, and the pews made way for bunks and lockers. After many visits to Golborne, I realised that outwardly it seemed to offer considerably less than many of the more orthodox establishments in the way of material comfort, and wondered why so many sought refuge at the Centre. For two reasons perhaps. One a practical consideration. In the centres set up by the local authorities, the homeless man had to present himself early in the evening if he was to be fortunate enough to secure himself a bed for the night. In the morning he was expected to help with the cleaning and other essential chores, and then he was told to leave. He has nowhere to go during the day and so just waits till five or six o'clock in the evening, when he will again be queuing at the same centre, or, having wandered too far from it, will be in search of a warm spot where he can sleep out the night. However, at Golborne, such a man was taken in and could stay indefinitely, leave when he liked and could consider himself a resident free to come and go in a small community. The other reason lay in the minister himself. His aim was to rekindle in each of his men some sense of their own dignity and importance. It was the individual, warm concern for the residents' well-being which raised Golborne high above any of the other centres for dossers.

There were the usual disappointments, naturally; a young homeless boy would spend three weeks there, helping with the chores without ever being asked, friendly and popular, and then suddenly disappear only to be found later in hospital suffering from an overdose. It was a base for many of the toughest criminal types. Some stayed for a few days, others for weeks. And some stayed longer, as helpers.

Golborne became another place for me to visit in the winter evenings. I used to frequent it two or three times a week to wash up the dinner plates or just to talk to the boys. With the young delinquents I was able to trace a pattern after a while. Most of them had been in trouble in their teens, and so were familiar with the Juvenile Courts and probation officers when they left school. They took a job, but after a few months they became bored and restless.

30

The advantages of a regular wage packet became insufficient compensation for the hours they put in, and there was no additional stimulus to hold them there, so they left. They drifted from one job to another; and from employment to unemployment; and were soon in trouble with the police again. Heavy drinking or drug-taking became part of their long-established social pattern. It all provided an escape from boredom. Soon they ran out of money and pilfering became their next excitement. It always ended in Borstal or prison.

My relationship with the lads took some months to establish. Some of them clearly looked upon me as a rather amusing curiosity and teased me incessantly about the way I spoke. This worried me at first and I thought it might prove a difficult barrier to cross, but I felt it was better than putting on a phoney accent which they might distrust. The more intelligent were perceptive enough to realise that I did not quite fit, and were highly suspicious. My presence, though, made no difference to the way they behaved. The language was well punctuated with the usual swear words and adjectives and as often as not, someone came out with a string of abuse just to see how I would react.

Having made a casual acquaintance with the boys, my problem became how to transform this superficial and fleeting relationship into one of greater depth and permanency without becoming too intimate. Gaining their acceptance was always the first step, but gaining their trust proved a very difficult second! Throughout my visits I concentrated on keeping the atmosphere personal and informal. On the whole the response was relaxed, but occasionally I met with abruptness and suspicion and a generally inflexible attitude; with this type it was not easy to communicate friendship.

One of these was Bob. Having been accepted by him as a regular visitor, I began to encourage him to talk factually about himself, especially about his home and family, to establish a relaxed and informal atmosphere. He was the eldest of five from a poor working-class family. His mother was a semi-invalid and his father also suffered from poor health. He was a strict authoritarian and Bob had resented the restrictions put on him. Whilst at school, when he was not playing truant, he produced inadequate work and lacked any kind of concentration. With another boy he became a peripheral member of a large and quite notorious group of youths involved in anti-social activities. He left school at fifteen and found a factory job. He found this both unpleasant and boring, and was eventually sacked. By now he had developed an ugly temper which he enjoyed losing; fighting was a regular outlet for his emotions. A couple of youth clubs were unable to cope with him and his own friends were transient. He worked up considerable hostility against any kind of authority. At sixteen he walked out of home never to return and roamed around England obtaining the odd job on a fair ground or on a building site. The rest of his time he spent in coffee bars or pubs. He resented anyone who had money, and his own philosophy was that money was the be-all and end-all of everything, with the implication that with remuneration one can do anything, everything. His attitude towards sex lacked respect: sexual intercourse was regarded as a matter of course at the first opportunity in any relationship. Later I was to discover that he had a wife somewhere and three children, though he swore only one was his. Since he left home he had been in and out of prison for pilfering and violence; when I met him he had just been discharged, having completed a four-year sentence for knifing a policeman. His attitude towards prison was particularly light-hearted, in fact he claimed to enjoy being 'inside', and it was a kindness on society's part to return him to prison, since the strain of living outside was so painful and intense.

I was to encounter many like Bob later. It became quite clear to me that repeated punishment was having less and less effect on the ex-convict and was serving almost the exact opposite purpose to that presumably intended, for it was neither deterring nor reforming him. It seemed to me axiomatic that the more often a man offended and went back to prison, the more clearly he was showing a need for care and understanding. Prison only covered behavioural or personality maladjustments with a layer of 'institutional neurosis', officially described as 'prisonisation'. Prison conditioned these men so that they were almost totally incapable of living outside. Was this because we set them standards that they were incapable of attaining and then followed it up by punishing them? Or was it that because their disabilities did not manifest themselves in physical symptoms or in any recognisable form, they drew no understanding or acceptance? I did not know the cause and I was equally unsure of the answers.

I persisted with my relationship with Bob despite the obvious suspicion and hostility. He refused to meet me in Golborne and so we met in a café in the Portobello Road at a prearranged time. This refusal was a self-recognition of his disreputable environment. Often he never turned up, or when he did, his behaviour was rude and insulting. I felt he was trying me and waiting to hear the familiar threat, "I'm not going to have anything more to do with you," but on these occasions I managed to hold my tongue and ignore him, which as often as not infuriated him more. Patience and perseverance over many months eventually proved their worth, though failure and success were relative concepts and I spent little time in considering them. When we did not meet in the coffee bar, we met in the pub where he would boast about how much drink he could take.

It took many meetings before he began to ask me for my help and advice. At first I was very cautious with my answers—I put out feelers. I tried not to dictate or deprive him of the right to self-determination, because I felt this would not help him to come to terms with himself or to develop a sense of responsibility towards his own affairs. When he consulted me about his problems I made no attempt to provide a ready-made solution or to pass moral judgement on the rights or wrongs of the situation. I tried to show him the involvements of his problems and the consequences of any action he might be contemplating. With Bob, I learnt that asking the right question was more important than knowing the right answer and more useful than any lecturing and moralising.

The first visible breakthrough came ten months after he left prison and five months after our first meeting at Golborne. I was sitting in Johnny's Café waiting for him; a couple of Teds were on the next table taking the micky out of me by referring to my 'posh' clothes and 'upper class' smell when Bob came in looking rather sheepish. He was smartly dressed and for the first time, shaved. But what took my breath away was the haircut. No longer did he look a troglodyte but a well-groomed young man. I wished that he had some false teeth, because the ugly gap when he smiled rather spoilt the effect.

"Bob, what a vast improvement!" I encouraged.

"I could take you anywhere now, couldn't I?"

"Indeed you could. To the best hotel."

"Yeah—Sal, I want to get a job."

"Good. Anything in mind?" I wanted to sound pleased but not enthusiastic, in case I frightened him off the idea.

"Well, I 'ad a job in a baker's once. I've got a mate who's said 'e'll fix me up workin' beside 'im in a bakery."

"Sounds admirable. Looking as you do, you'd get any job you applied for, but that sounds a splendid idea." I wanted to ask when he was thinking of starting, but I refrained. I was glad I had.

"My mate thinks 'e can get me in on Monday. You think that's all right? And when I get a bit of lolly I'll take you out."

"That would be lovely, I'll look forward to that. Meanwhile here's a packet of cigarettes." It gave him the opening he wanted.

"Er ... Sal, could you lend me a quid to see me over?"

"Okay, as long as it doesn't all go on drink." I knew it would, but it did not worry me. I had given him a small amount previous to this and it had been lavishly spent in the pub, but I felt that our relationship was not established enough to refuse him his demand without an almighty scene and a final break-up.

Bob took the job in the bakery, and twice a week I met him after work, in the pub. Initially, the mere fact of having a job boosted his ego, not to mention the wages. Expansively, he insisted on taking me out for meals, and often we went to the cinema. Once or twice I brought along a girl-friend so that he would become accustomed to having females around him without having to think of going to bed with them. On our outings he was always the gentleman, well-mannered and protective, yet he was still very moody and very quick-tempered. Drink was still his downfall and he was always ready to take on anyone who was prepared to fight. If someone refused to fight him he went into tantrums like a spoilt child, though next morning when he had sobered up, he would have forgotten all about it.

The second barrier was broken three months after he had taken his bakery job.

"Sal, will yer 'elp me?"

"If I can. What's the trouble?"

"I want to go home and see my old lady again." This took the wind out of my sails.

"Splendid! But why do you want my help?"

"Well, I don't think my old man'll have me in the house, having not been in touch in the last five years like, and I was wonderin' like if you could go and see them first?"

"Why not go together one day?" I felt it would be better if he managed this step alone, with me just behind him to support him.

"Would you do that then?"

"Of course. Where do they live?"

"West Byfleet, near Woking in Surrey. We can get a Green Line bus all the way. When can you get off from work?"

"Next Thursday?" I said, glancing through my diary.

"Okay. Meet you at Hammersmith at ten-thirty."

"It's a date." I was about to say it was time I went when he thrust ten pounds into my hand. "What's this for?"

"Keep it for me, will you? Stop me spendin' it on booze."

"As you wish. Why not start a post office account?"

"No," he answered defiantly. "You keep it. I trust you."

"All right if that's what you want."

I departed with mixed feelings. Had I been too gullible? Did he really have parents out at West Byfleet? Or was he just wanting to get me out into the country? After all, Dave of Golborne had often said about Bob that I was playing with fire – was I? To date it had all been too good to be true; was there any evil intent behind his improvements? Was I just another sucker?

I was at the bus stop on Thursday as agreed. Together, we travelled to West Byfleet. Alone we crossed a canal bridge towards a row of council houses. We stopped outside one of them. Bob's confidence deserted him. "You go and face the old man first," he urged.

Leaving him at the front gate, I walked up the path not knowing quite what to expect. Having tapped on the front door with no result, I edged it open. I was standing in a minute kitchen.

"Come in, dear, what can I do for you? I'm through here."

I looked into the adjoining room and saw a vast figure bulging over a chair; despite her size, her face was haggard and lined, a face that had tasted poverty and suffering.

"I'm sorry to disturb you, my name's Sally. You must be Mrs. H. Could I talk to you for a minute?" I noticed another figure in the corner. He was long and lanky like Bob but his features were softer; his eyes were tired and his expression was one of weary resignation. He greeted me suspiciously.

"I'll be quite frank with you," I began. "I've come down about your son, Bob. I've been seeing a lot of him lately and he's doing very well for himself. He's in a good job now." There was no reaction.

"I thought 'e was in prison," his father said eventually.

"No, he's been out nearly a year now and is really making a go of it."

"Believe that when I see it!"

"As a matter of fact you can. Bob's outside." There was a silence and Mr. H. turned as white as a sheet. "If you turn him away, you could be doing as much damage as signing

36

a court order. You might be causing irreparable damage. Let him prove himself as he has done to me," I exhorted. Mrs. H. glanced nervously across at her husband who was in turn clenching his fists with anger.

"He's spent four years paying his debts," I went on hastily, "he's squared it up, now he's wanting to square it up with you. Give him that chance. He is your son."

"Let me see the boy, Dad. It's been a long time," Mrs. H. burst out.

He stared at her astonished. "Since when did you concern yourself about your eldest?" She began to cry. I sat like a stuffed rabbit feeling utterly helpless while they argued. Words were useless when fighting bitterness.

"Let me see 'im. You don't have to," Mrs. H. wept.

"Stop your crying." He sat puffing his pipe; only the monotonous tick of the clock broke the silence. "Well, since he's here, he'd better come in," he said gruffly.

Outside, Bob was like an excited child, hopping from one foot to the other.

"Come on," I said, "they're waiting for you." He followed behind as I led him into the drawing-room. His father got to his feet and they faced each other like a couple of angry bulls. Mr. H. broke it.

"Hello, son."

"Hello, Ma." Silence and then Bob put out his hand to his father.

"Hello, Dad. Sorry I haven't written." His father made no move to reciprocate the gesture. I saw Bob's ears go red, and his eyes began to narrow. His mother caught her breath, and I bit my lip. They were both too big for me to hold from fighting. Then the man took the pipe from his lips and laid it down on the mantlepiece. Grudgingly he extended his hand. I breathed again. "You'll stay to lunch, won't you?" he said.

Bob began to visit them once a month, both men making great efforts to accept each other as they were. Whenever he went down there, he always took a large cake that he baked for the family. The ice had been broken, and each visit became easier and more enjoyable for them all. I prided myself on my success. A few months later I was to receive a jolt. It was just another lesson I was to learn.

Bob was very demanding on both time and emotion. He expected me to give him all my attention and became extremely jealous if I lavished any interest on anyone else. Having been so successful with him so far, and brought about what I thought was a 'drastic cure', I rather sat back preening myself. I was so confident that I had him at my fingertips that I became careless.

I had met up with another social worker called Duncan who was a male nurse in a mental home. He was interested in my work at Golborne and asked me to take him along to see it. I agreed. It was thoughtless of me and a very grave mistake. After work we made our way to the Portobello Road, and as I passed Johnny's Café I noticed Bob out of the corner of my eye. His eyes were narrowed on Duncan. Even then I was blind to the danger signals. Knowing well that if Bob wanted to see me he would come out to make his presence known, I walked on to the Centre. We passed the evening talking to the 'boys' and washing up the dinner plates; half-way through, Bob came in. Without acknowledging me he went and sat at the far table. I smiled at him from where I was sitting, but only received a scowl, so I made no further attempt to communicate with him. I think possibly that was another mistake too.

At eleven Duncan and I said our farewells to Dave and began to amble towards the tube station in Ladbroke Grove. Suddenly Bob and one of his mates appeared from nowhere. They blocked our path and Bob began to scream with rage. "You f . . . hypocrite. You bloody bitch." From the wallet I had given him he extracted my letters to him and tore them into little pieces and threw them at us. I quickened the pace. They followed right behind. We bought two tickets and started down the stairs, Bob still shouting after me. A few people turned to see where the filthy language was coming from. Something hit me on the shoulder. It was the diary I had given Bob. It fell to the ground, and with his mate Pete on his heels he came up to us. Silently I began to pray, for I realised Bob meant business. "Pick it up," he ordered me. I took no notice. He grabbed me by the coat. Duncan made as if to defend me, but Pete threw him back by the seat. "Pick it up!" I stared in disgust at him. He spat in my face and let me go. I said nothing but took out a handkerchief and wiped my face. He went on shouting obscene language at me again and threatened to knock Duncan's head off.

A train came in and its door slid open. Duncan and I, relieved, boarded, but to my horror so did Bob and Pete. I looked around; there were a few girls opposite us and a couple of men at the other end. I scanned Bob's waist line for a bulge. As far as I could see he had no knife on him, but his fists were clenched, and his face was full of hatred. After a while, he began to tremble and then it was over before I realised it. He had Duncan, who was half his size, on his feet and was beating him round the head. The girls opposite screamed and rushed to the other end of the tube, and to my utter disgust so did the men. Suddenly I saw red and in my fury threw all caution to the wind. Head down, I bull-dozed my way between the two grappling men. I had no inhibitions about how I fought. I went for Bob like a cat, kicking, biting and punching. I felt Pete pounce on me. Somehow I threw him off. We were drawing into a station. "Duncan, get off!" I screamed. I felt that I could handle them better without him, and that if he remained they would really hurt him. He hesitated and the doors were closing. "Duncan, do as you're told, get off." It was not the time to act the heroic cavalier. I saw him crawl on to the platform; how hurt he was, I did not know. I was pushed back into my seat. I heard Bob giving Pete directions to disembark at the next station and wait for the next train, hoping that Duncan was on it, and that if he himself had not returned in two hours' time to Golborne, he was to come with some of the lads over to St. John's Wood and look my address up in the telephone book and raid the house.

I wondered who he thought was going to call the police. The compartment had emptied, and we were now alone. I was too empty and deflated to talk. I guessed that now that Duncan had gone, and now that he had let off steam, Bob would not touch me. My main worry now was to get rid of him before we reached St. John's Wood and I reached home, so that he would not know where I lived. At the stop before St. John's Wood I got out, Bob followed. I began to walk slowly, taking the long way round, keeping to the main roads as a precaution. He followed a few yards behind.

"Come and talk. Don't follow me like a shadow." I stopped to allow him to catch up, but he refused and stood still. I shrugged my shoulders and walked on. It was cold and I began to shiver. I wondered if Duncan had had the sense to go a different way home or if he was in hospital or at the police station.

"Shall we walk a bit faster? It's a bit chilly." I explained my movements in case he became suspicious of my intentions. A police car drove by; I pretended I had not seen it.

"Go on, call' em," he shouted at me. I took no notice.

"Go on, you want me back in nick. Why don't you call 'em?"

"I can't now anyway. They've gone; and even if I could, I wouldn't."

"You bein' soft on me? Don't waste it, mate." I walked on. Whatever happened, I would not be the one to call the police. If I did I knew he would be sent back to prison because of his previous records of violence. It would ruin everything that he had built. We were passing some road works now, just going into St. John's Wood, and I was working out where I was going to tramp next—anywhere but home. Suddenly something hard zoomed past me, grazing my head. It was a workman's oil lantern. As it crashed to the ground, Bob hit me on the back of my neck. I fell to the ground and lay there pretending I was unconscious. The fact that he had hit me was far more painful to me than the actual blow. The pavement was hard and cold, and I found it rather boring lying there, so I groaned myself to apparent consciousness and got to my feet. Bob was leaning against a wall seemingly unconcerned. "Still not going to call the cops?" he asked.

"Nope, not now, not never; so I should stop wasting your time trying to make me. I'm going home. I'm tired." Determinedly I marched away.

Eventually, at the end of our road, I turned to Bob. "I live down here. I only hope my father hasn't called the police himself to search for me. I suggest you go back to Golborne and stop your friends coming out here. I hope you've enjoyed your evening, I haven't. In fact I've been sickened by the whole affair. You must be proud of yourself. I'll see you next Monday at the usual time, but let's not have another demonstration like this. Good night."

I turned my back and went into the house. As I was opening the front door, I heard the telephone ring. Well, this would wake them if they were not already awake. I heard my brother's voice: "No, she's not in. I haven't a clue where she is, and at this time of night, I don't really care. Good night." He slammed the receiver down, and muttering under his breath, went back to bed. Thank heavens he had answered it and not my father. Quietly I slipped upstairs. It was wonderful to be safely in bed. Only then was I aware of how frightened I had been.

My door burst open and all six foot two inches of my brother blocked the aperture. "What the hell are you up to? Don't your bloody friends sleep? According to this one on now, it's a matter of life and death. I told him to ring back in the morning, but he said it's urgent. Get him off the bloody line will you, so I can get some sleep." Fuming, he bounced out. I made my way to the telephone wondering what had happened now.

It was Pete, ringing from St. John's Wood Station. Bob had not turned up at the specified time, and Pete and his mates had come to find out why. I managed with difficulty to persuade them that I had not split to the cops, that as far as I knew Bob should be back at Golborne by now. With a final threat that, if he wasn't there I would 'know all about it', Pete rang off.

I retired to bed with my heart in my mouth. Somehow I dozed off. But every now and then I went to the window and

41

drew my curtains back. There was nothing to see, and the morning arrived without further mishap. But with it came questions and abuses from my brother, and much explaining to my parents for the late hour I had come in. I lied my way clear.

The next time I saw Bob he was subdued with shame but could not bring himself to apologise, nor even mention it; I was thankful that I had remained impassive to his dares and threats, for it saved our relationship as well as his freedom. From that episode I learnt to think in terms of prevention rather than cure. With a year behind me at Golborne I had proved that sympathy, understanding and genuine concern for an individual's condition, in contrast to the cynicism and despair which were so characteristic of many, was half the battle in adjusting the delinquent. Bob loved and respected me far more after that dreadful night than he had done before. In fact, when I went into hospital a few weeks later with a bad back, a nurse said a very strange thing to me. "That man was out there again. I told him he could come in and see you, but he seemed a bit bashful."

"What man?" I asked, staggered.

"Hasn't anyone told you? There's a man who comes along at eight every evening and catches one of the nurses going off to find out how you are. He's fairly tall, without any front teeth and rather grubby looking. He sits at the bottom of the stairs eating his sandwiches waiting for one of us off the ward." I laughed.

"That's Bob. Do tell him to come up next time you see him."

The following morning she came and saw me. "I did as you asked, but he was quite adamant about it. He said he thought he might let you down amongst your posh visitors so he sends his love and asked me to give you this." She handed me a transistor radio. "Oh, yes, and he says, don't worry, he didn't nick it!" The nurse's eyebrows went up, but she made no further comment.

CHAPTER FOUR

ONE evening when I biked over to Golborne, just before the Bob episode, I bumped into Dave going out. He was wearing a suit, which was unusual.

"Hello, hello, and who's the lucky bird, Dave?"

"Don't be daft," he replied self-consciously, "I'm going to a meeting. I've got to give a talk on Golborne."

"Sounds good publicity. Who to?"

"Simons?"

"Who are Simons?"

"From the Simon Community."

"What is the Simon Community?"

"It's a community of our sort of lads here."

"Why Simon?"

"After Simon of Cyrene, who helped carry the cross of our Lord."

"Ugh! Religious?"

"No, undenominational like us, though the founder is a Roman Catholic, I believe. Look, why don't you come along to the meeting with me instead of asking all these questions, and see for yourself? You can help me out with the talk, too."

I had nothing to lose, so I agreed. Little did I know the extent to which I was committing myself.

The meeting was held in a large terraced house just off the Harrow Road. I was introduced to the owner, Helen Jacobs, as she sat buttering sandwiches and making coffee. One by one strangers came in to whom I was politely introduced. About fifteen had arrived when the chairman opened the meeting in front of a glowing fire, spread-eagled in an armchair. "The Central London Group's minutes for the last meeting, please, Miss Dixon." I was told later that the Companions of Simon were divided into area Groups. Most of the meeting was double-dutch to me, but the interval was first class—plenty of tasty grub and stacks of coffee. Dave contributed his piece after the interval, and I filled in a few gaps that he left out. The meeting came to a close and more food and more coffee was produced. It was an excellent evening.

As we left Dave said, "You know, you ought to go and visit a Simon house. You'd find it most interesting. Go and see their house in Camden Town. It's called St. Joseph's."

The following evening I paid a call on St. Joseph's. It was one of many shabby terraced houses running geometrically east to west. The exterior looked decayed and ready for demolition. The door was open, so I boldly walked in. My first fleeting impression was that it reminded me of Piccadilly Circus; there was a congestion of bodies in a rather dark and dingy corridor. The wallpaper was peeling off, and the floors unswept. Young men swaggered around in creased Italian-cut suits and winkle-picker shoes, whilst the older folk wore grubby and worn clothes that were either too small or too big for them. Most of them were unshaved and obviously took no care of their appearance whatsoever. No one had taken any notice of my entrance, so casually, with an air of 'I belong here too', I nosed around.

The small kitchen was a continuation of the corridor, where a couple of boys were busy washing up. To its right I found the dining-room where a group of men sat mournfully staring at the cluttered table. I received an occasional hostile glance, but no one questioned me or greeted me. I found the front room was an office where another group of men were sitting on either the beds or the desk or wherever they could place themselves in comfort. A few were on the floor.

"Can I help you, Miss?" a tall, balding man asked.

I introduced myself. He shook my hand. "I'm Len Green and I run the joint in a sort of way."

The door burst open, and in came a paunchy young man with receding hair. He wore thick-rimmed glasses which gave him the appearance of an academic. He had a certain air of confidence about him, and was wearing a good-looking sports coat. Somehow I knew he was not a down-and-out.

"Everything all right, Len?" He had a pleasant-sounding voice.

"Yup, except the Berkshire probation officers have asked us if we'd take in an epileptic grave-digger. And the grocers say if they don't get paid within the next two days, we'll have to go somewhere else for our groceries."

"What, another?"

"Yes, and this is Sally from Golborne. She's just come to sus. the joint."

"An enemy in the camp! How are you? I'm Pat Egan, supposedly the bursar, but since we have no money to burse I fall short of this rank." I liked him. "Have you seen round the place yet?"

"I've only just come."

"Well, allow me to give you a conducted tour. Incidentally, have you eaten, because I haven't. Len, what's cooking?"

"You're too late Pat, it's all been eaten. Though there's plenty of bread and cheese." Pat turned up his nose with distaste.

"Check, be a good lad and pop down the road and buy two lots of fish and chips." A middle-aged lanky body un- wound himself from the bed, and, talking to himself, sauntered out. "Right; coffee?" There was a murmur of approval at his suggestion. We went out into the kitchen where we could talk more quietly without interruption.

That evening, over the fish and chips, I learnt a lot about the Simon Community. The more Pat talked, the more I liked what I heard. Here, at last, was what I had been in search of for all these months. "Our philosophy is com- plete permissiveness and tolerance for the next man," Pat explained in a somewhat pontificating manner. "His past means nothing to us; we are only interested in his future. To accept people as they are, and not as they were. To for- give and forget." I knew Simon was for me, because we shared the same vision and the same principles. But I never realised just then how much I was to become involved.

The Simon Community, generally referred to as 'Simon', was a new experimental venture in care for the social inadequate. It was founded in the autumn of 1963 by Anton Wallich Clifford, on the ideal that condemning men and women to homelessness, prison or mental hospitals for whatever they had done, or failed to do, was not the answer to the problems of our society or of the individuals themselves.

It was a ten-year-old dream before Anton was able to sow the first seeds of Simon. In those days he was just a progressive probation officer in London who recognised the increasing problem of social inadequacy. Thus it was that in 1961 he helped found the Voluntary Hostels Conference (now the National Association of Voluntary Hostels) as a 'front-line' movement to further this recognition and to assist the acute problem of accommodation and care arising directly from the social isolation and apathy of the misfit. He watched with marked interest the pioneers such as Merfyn Turner and Austin Williams, of Norman House and St. Martin of Tours respectively, establish themselves, and other similar units get off the ground. But there were still too few to meet the increasing demand made on them and, moreover, their effectiveness was confined to an upper stratum of homeless offenders and patients. By statistics, Anton proved that for the hard core of severely socially crippled men and women – the persistent recidivists, the hospital 'social problems'—short-term work or care was failing. Also he felt very strongly that the existing statutory services were ineffectual, and tended to aggravate rather than diminish the problem by increasing the feeling of rejection; he was sure that many could be helped to live relatively useful lives, without offending or demanding from society, provided they were given a protected environment, with unpressurised, long-term care and individual attention.

To meet this challenge, and to spearhead the mission to the misfit, the Simon Community Trust was created under Anton's directorship and was registered with the Charity Commissioners; soon Simon was to make a home for hundreds, as opposed to a temporary haven or just another doss-house. It was to care for the inadequate, the alcoholic, the drug addict, the ex-convict, the meths drinker, the mentally disturbed and the homeless. Simon was to welcome home the rejects of our society, the forgotten bundles of humanity.

But the road to Simon was not just being a concerned social worker. It took hard work, courage and, above all, faith. In November 1962, Anton had to make the decision of his life. Either to remain in the square orthodox world of our stodgy middle-class society, living well and comfortably as a middle-aged bachelor, with a secure office job with plenty of future; or to make a definite break from society and security and join the undesirable world of the un-wanted. He put away his bowler hat and umbrella and quietly departed from the affluent society he was used to. Clad in shoddy clothes he moved to Southampton to assist Father Pat Murphy-O'Connor to open Dismas House, a half-way house for discharged prisoners. Here for two years, whilst initiating Simon, he worked amongst the criminals of our time, and made contact with the undesirables whom he felt could have a place in his brain-child.

Meanwhile, he and his trustees, who represented a very influential cross-section of well-known personalities, continued to solicit prayer, support and financial help towards the ultimate object of launching a country estate for his future community. The dream almost came true when negotiations were in progress to buy an estate in Sussex which would accommodate fifty people. Capital of £14,000 had been raised by way of guarantee, and Christian Action had promised help. Initially the plan envisaged a home farm, a half-way house, an alcoholic lodge and a system of family cottages. But Anton's plans were halted after the local press had given adverse publicity to his ideas of starting a community in the district for down-and-outs. The local council fought him and won.

A year later, in May 1964, quietly and inconspicuously, the Simon Community opened St. Joseph's, a House of

47

Hospitality, in North West London. It started with three contacts Ánton had brought up from Dismas House, and from that first day the doors were kept open twenty-four hours a day. Between the three of them, articles were written, posters were painted, people were notified and house-to-house begging organised. This all-out drive on promotion by Anton and his trustees brought Simon into the public eye, and support, both practical and financial, rapidly grew. Anton and Sidney B.S., treasurer and a trustee, attended one-night stands at public meetings all over the country. They talked as they had never talked before, inspiring and enthralling their audiences with the ideals and needs of Simon. In a very short period of time, its methods and philosophy were proved to be acceptable for the social misfit, and qualified social workers were recommending their problem clients to us.

The essential feature of St. Joe's was the permissive regime and high degree of tolerance. There were no rules; the men were allowed to come and go as they liked, and were not required to get up or go to bed at any fixed hour. During the day it was hoped that some would be willing to do some of the essential chores. If not, then they did not get done. Meals were continuous as long as the cook was prepared to supply them to anyone who wanted to eat, though bread and cheese, being the easiest to prepare, was the staple diet. Yet sometimes I have known the cook to get up in the middle of the night when he has heard some poor cold tramp come in. Conversation and discussions about community business were often held with the inmates for, by doing so, Anton felt it gave an air of belonging and a feeling of participation, which in turn gave a sense of 'home'. As a member was never asked to leave, it gave him an additional sense of security, so essential to people who have experienced years of rejection and who had finally rejected society themselves.

Another of Anton's philosophies was that to persist in the ethic that work was the only respectable way of living was merely creating further conflicts. He felt strongly that members who wanted to work should wait until they were absolutely ready, otherwise they would only relapse, which would give them a further sense of failure. He encouraged them by telling them they were doing a good job working for each other, and in keeping a self-contained community. This proved true, for in time they began to take an active responsibility for each other, and by doing so they began to interact in the group in a positive and out-going way. As this developed they began to lose their apathy and also their identification with their former life. With the security came self-confidence and eventually a new equilibrium was found. This was important, for they must regain their own self-respect before they could modify their behaviour. Again this is where Anton's philosophy differed from that of the other organisations; he felt that the best way of helping them was to meet them on their own level, and not expect them to meet him on his terms and standards. Thus it was that Joe's was never particularly spruced up, but just rough-and-ready like the inmates.

The Simon houses became a kind of pipe-line. From the permissive and rather dirty reception centres of St. Joe's and St. Antony's at Rochester, the boys were automatically moved to Simonrise at Rochester. Here a higher standard of living was exercised. In contrast to the bare wooden table with a meal of bread and cheese for anyone who should wander in at St. Joe's, the inmates of Simonrise sat down to two-course meals from off tablecloths. No one went to Simonrise from off the street, they had to pass through St. Joe's or St. Antony's first. From Simonrise, they moved on to Simonwell, a farm purposely situated in a very rural part of Kent. Here a very ordered family life was maintained. Meals were excellent and always to time. They enjoyed inviting guests down, guests whom they could entertain in their own home, and it brought them in touch with the 'world'. During the day everyone had a job to do in the house or on the farm. It was interesting to find that those who had progressed up this pipe-line and were now well instated at the farm, were critical of the state of St. Joe's and St. Antony's. They felt it lowered the tone of Simon! This was a good sign—they were taking an interest in their fellow-men and so becoming viable members of a community. It was interesting to see that they had forgotten that at one stage they had been part of St. Joe's. In this way they had raised their own standards without actually realising it.

Anton was Simon's only full-time trained social worker. He took his own lads who had come up from skid-row level and completed the pipe-line of houses, and trained them to run the new houses. For instance a young epileptic ex-convict was house leader at St. Joe's, whilst an alcoholic ran St. Antony's and a homosexual kept the peace at the farm; a highly reputed safe-breaker who had once 'cased a joint' and got away with £30,000, was in charge of Simonrise. This was another of Anton's controversial ideas: he believed in creating the situation by putting them in a house and leaving the 'group' to help itself as a group of individuals. Thus the drug addict was looking after the alcoholic, and the alcoholic looking after the epileptic.

So it was that when I landed on the scene, Simon had a self-contained community with four viable houses catering for up to twenty-five occupants in each. In each house there were the hard-core Simon workers who had previously passed through the mill and, instead of returning to society, lived on in Simon in voluntary poverty and shared the same cramped conditions and insecurity of the down-and-out, only receiving one pound pocket money a week and keep. Thus the caring and the cared for were living together on an equal footing.

Brian is one of the many success stories in Simon. At the age of two his mother put him in a children's home because she could not be bothered to look after him (his father had walked out some time ago). He was brought up in this children's home until the age of fifteen, school-leaving time, when his mother suddenly turned up and demanded him back. She packed him off to work every day to bring in the rent money. Being so unsettled and resenting his mother's behaviour, he drifted from one job to another. For fun he made abusive anonymous telephone calls to people. He was picked up and put on probation for three years. A year later he was picked up again for carrying a stolen butcher's knife on him—further probation. Months later he pinched a bicycle and when the police charged him he tried to lie his way out. He was put temporarily in a mental home and then moved to a rehabilitation centre. On his release he began making more anonymous telephone calls, and made small amounts of money by breaking and entering private houses. He was caught and sent to Borstal. He took up his old ways on discharge and was returned to prison.

He drifted to Simon after his third prison discharge. By chance there was no one prepared to cook in Joe's at the time, and Brian was offered the position. Like the others he moved to Simonrise and thence to the farm, where he was given a taste of being deputy house leader. Anton brought him back to St. Joe's to become Assistant Organising Secretary to the Companions. When Simon House, the office in the city, was opened, he was promoted to office manager and became Anton's right hand man. With specialised care and attention, Anton managed to produce the best out of this boy. But the story does not end here, for Brian was not a Simon hard-core member because he was still drawing his £3 10s. a week National Assistance Board money. The community hard-core members were not registered with N.A.B., as they were classed as working in the community, which paid their stamps and pocket money. But the day did come when Brian, on his own volition, came to Anton and asked if he could become a hard-core Simon worker and like the other workers just draw one pound.

Of course, Anton had his failures too. John, an alcoholic, an ex-commissioned officer in the Army, and from a well-to-do Irish family, was at one time in charge of one of our houses. For six months he ran the house brilliantly, keeping it in order and maintaining a happy atmosphere among the men, which is an incredibly difficult combination when one is dealing with maladjusted people with personality conflicts. Suddenly, for no apparent reason, he broke. With thirty-six pounds of the house's petty cash money, he walked out. We did nothing about it. We did not call in the police or go in search of him, despite knowing his hide-outs. We just hoped and prayed he would come back to us in one piece. We waited for news.

Two weeks later we received a telephone call from Bow Street magistrates' court; a probation officer there, knowing he was one of our lads, gave us the tip-off that he was coming up in front of the court that day on a charge of being drunk and disorderly. We dashed over and bailed him out. We took him back to St. Joe's where we dried him out. We never mentioned the missing money. Why should we? It was over, and he had spent it, so what would have been the purpose? Obviously he was ashamed of himself and more so because we were prepared to have him back and not reject him for his failure. It was wonderful having him back, but it always was when we received a lost sheep back to the fold. In time John regained his self-respect and dignity, and his old confidence returned. Within three months he was back as house leader, running it smoothly and honestly. Often we were to lose money or things, but this was of little importance. We were dealing with failures, the throw-outs of other organisations, the 'impossible' cases and the 'no hope' cases —we never expected success.

To relieve the forlornness, failure and desperation afflicting someone unwanted for years, warmth and understanding and sympathy were as essential to a Simon Home as a roof, four walls and a bed. Usually the house leader could provide this, having moved through the same sufferings and experiences himself. Of course, Anton was always on call for advice or to deal with any house emergency that was beyond the control of the house leader. Anton, himself, was peripatetic. He moved around the houses, staying sometimes just overnight, sometimes for a week. But he was in constant touch with the other houses. One day he was in Rochester when the house leader rang up to say one of the boys had gone berserk and, having smashed all the windows on the second floor, had now locked himself in the lavatory. Anton, the only man knowing the case history of the culprit, was the only one in the position to deal with him. Whether he could be talked down, threatened or black-mailed out, or whether sheer force was the only answer, only Anton knew. Of course the house leaders got to know the characters they were looking after fairly well after a time, and often learnt to deal with them when they became diffi-cult without having to contact Anton. The latter liked them on the whole to deal with the situation themselves for it forced them to face their responsibility and use their initia-tive and thus sharpened the 'conception of self'.

Simon was providing a service of accommodation and security and a therapeutic environment for those who fell beneath the Statutes. Simon was solving the problem of the down-and-out. Many said that this was already being done by the Welfare State; this Simon did not deny, but the exist-ing provision the Welfare State made for this type of person was not adequate and not the right kind of treatment. Simon, being a small and flexible organisation, was attempt-ing to create a more 'tolerating' environment for society's deviants. When I came into Simon it was not old enough for me to draw any real conclusions about its methods, but at least I found it was trying to solve the problem of meeting the needs of the misfit in society, and these were the were the people I cared about.

I had an excellent job that I really enjoyed when I decided to go full-time into Simon and subsequently into social work. I was earning nearly £900 a year, plus travelling allowance, and thus I was able to buy plenty of food and cigarettes for my dossers. I made the decision after my first meeting with Anton; in fact it was strange how we were thrown together to enable me to make it.

I was now visiting St. Joe's regularly, but Anton was away in Naples seeing Father Borelli's work, so I had never met him. One evening I appeared at St. Joe's straight from work, looking rather smart, only to find cameramen occupying the rooms. I grabbed Check. "What's going on here, are you making a film?"

"Nah, Sal, blooming television people,' he grumbled.

I settled down out of the way to watch as they interviewed Pat. At the end Pat turned to me and said, "Sal, be a sport and go and give Kim his pills—here's the key to the medicine chest. Don't let him con you into giving him more than two." As I went out I heard Tim, the producer enquire about me. When I returned, Pat called me over. "How would you like to appear on television? Tim here thinks it would add a bit of glamour!" I was very chuffed at the idea.

And so it was that I appeared on television talking about the Simon Community, without having ever met its founder and director. Anton managed to return from Naples just in time to see the programme; simultaneously I landed in hospital with my old back injury. Anton saw the programme at his mother's home, and as soon as it was finished he was on the telephone to Pat, enquiring about this young dynamic girl who had spoken with such sincerity and enthusiasm. Directly he made preparations to return to London to meet me.

As he walked up the ward, out of visiting hours, I recognised him from his photographs. I was thrilled to meet this great man. He plonked himself on my bed and from the very beginning I felt as if I had known him all my life. He sat with me for over an hour, we swapped stories and experiences and giggled together like a couple of school-children; one would not have thought there were twenty years between us, the way we gassed and shared the same wonderful vision. I think he was as impressed with me as I was with him. I thought the world of him in just that one meeting. He had great ideas for me, and when he had finished reading some of my articles, insisted that I became a sub-editor to his monthly paper. He left me with my imagination reeling with ideas and prospects for the two of us working together.

It was three months before I was in circulation again, and the first action I took was to give in my notice at my job; the second was to appear at Anton's office to tell him I had come to work for him full-time. That afternoon we discussed plans for expanding the Simon Community, we discussed the administrative affairs, the community problems, we discussed everything under the sun. It was extraordinary how similar our approach to the social problems of the country were; we were on the same wave-length throughout. That night I skipped all the way home, so happy that my dreams of really helping these people, not just by giving them coffee and fags every night, but by providing a roof and a home, had come true. Once back at home, I was brought back to reality with a bump as I plucked up courage to tell my parents I had thrown my job in, to work voluntarily with Anton amongst dossers and criminals. To give father his due, he took it fairly well, though I know he disapproved. I expected a rocket, but fortunately he was too caught up in his own work and problems to really digest the full meaning of it. Later we were to have many rows about it, eventually ending in disaster by my walking out and causing my parents a great amount of unhappiness. So I came into the Simon Community as a fully-fledged worker, as Anton's personal assistant and eventually his co-director.

For the first month I went everywhere with him; whether it was to do a food run to one of the houses, to do a 'skipper' on a bomb-site, to edit the monthly paper *Simonstar*, or to go and visit a man in prison. I learnt how to deal with people and to love them despite their failings and faults. As a team we worked well; he passed down his knowledge and in return I gave him young fresh ideas. If we could have remained detached it might have worked; yet the Simon Community could not have worked on an impersonal uninvolved basis, for we relied on personal contact and identification. At the beginning we went from strength to strength and Anton and I shared the privilege of shouldering the many burdens; as his confidence grew in me he gave me more work. Soon I was touring the country giving lectures, or if he was away on tour I would remain at the office and hold the fort that end, coping with house troubles, administrative problems and publicity. Because of Anton's complete faith in my ability to cope, he made it clear to all our hundred-odd inmates that in his absence I was in control. This could have proved terribly awkward as I was still a teenager, still wet behind the ears, but thankfully I won the confidence of the house leaders who trusted Anton's judgement implicitly. Whatever Anton said went without question, and when he was absent my leadership was never disputed.

I have never worked so hard in all my life as I did for Anton and his cause, and I loved every minute of it. Often we only managed a couple of hours' sleep a night, other times we just worked on, not knowing whether it was night or day. We drove ourselves on and on, completely hypnotised by our vision of having a self-contained and self-supporting community. Our work was not in vain, for after two years of existence, Simon had six viable houses in operation and a fully-staffed office in the City. We still refused to have any trained social workers in, and each house and the office were all manned by the lads themselves. Anton had succeeded towards half his ambition, we were a self-contained community, but alas! we were hardly self-supporting. Neither of us being accountants, nor particularly efficient in administration, we had no idea how much money we were losing. Anton never wanted to be stuck behind an office desk and was the first to admit he was pretty useless there, but since there was no one else apart from me, he took his share of the burden. Nevertheless, it did not stop us from doing a night's 'skipper' on Waterloo Station. Having changed from our office clothes into our dosser's outfits we would make our way to the station, our pockets filled with cigarettes for the lads, and sit amongst them on the benches talking to them, finding out their problems and needs. There was one memorable occasion when both Anton and I, with little Neil, were thrown off the station as suspicious characters! It was a great joke amongst the lads for months!

Our real work on the 'coal-face' took place in Simonlight. This was in Cable Street, Stepney, known as London's 'Little Harlem'. It was a shelter in a row of gutted houses and dingy cafés, linked to the bomb-sites of the East End. During the day, the crumbling street was like a graveyard. At night it came to life. Prostitutes appeared, and Negroes, half stoned, waited in the doorways for their friends; and when the rain fell social derelicts, having brewed their lethal drinks, crawled from their bomb-sites to hug the shadow of the walls. We opened Simonlight to them. It was dirty but warm; no questions were asked, instead we handed them a bowl of soup or a cup of tea and a slice of bread. We slept them anywhere and everywhere; we welcomed them with their bottle of meths or 'jake'. To many it was the first real home they had ever known. At the weekends we slept up to a hundred; they sprawled on top of each other in their clothes and boots, lying on soiled mattresses. Their faces flushed and fiery red with meths, they lay there with their bottles at their sides. The sweet sickening stench would sting our nostrils at first until we grew immune to it. Often we would go out in the middle of the night and fetch those unable to walk without aid, and carry them back. All night, hungry and thirsty men knocked on the door for a slice of bread and soup. No one was refused. Other nights we would go out with soup to the bomb-sites and feed them, or down to the caves and into the drains by the docks. Anton was happiest here amongst the men on the bomb-sites. He was a good listener and they appreciated that. Often we found ourselves bringing back the same wreck as the night before, and we always went through the same procedure with them. First we would have to feed them, mostly on Complan, because they could not hold down solids after drinking 'jake' all day. Then we would wash them down and tend their burns and injuries before carrying them to the basement where we would put them in the 'pit' to sleep it off.

The first man I ever felt I had done something worthwhile for was C. For four months I had performed this ritual of going out and looking for him and every time had helped him back to Simonlight and fed him Complan with a teaspoon; every morning after soup he shuffled out in search of

57

more drink, and I knew I would be looking for him again that night. When he left next morning, he never smiled or said thank you, and often I would feel despondent, and that I was wasting my time. Then one day I picked C. up and he was very ill; the meths was burning him up fast. I got him back to our shelter and for two days I sat with him as he died. I held his hand, hoping that at one minute or another he would become conscious enough to realise that he was not alone and that someone cared. I fed him regularly and bathed down his sweating body and I prayed. When he rallied two days later, I was still there and he knew it. His eyes were weak as the result of the meths so he could not see me, but his grip on my hand tightened. For the first time since I had known him he smiled and said, "Girl, yer the first person who's loved me." I wept many a tear when a few days later he died. Yet amongst these boys death was not a tragedy but a relief.

Anton and Simon were synonymous. Without Anton there would be no Simon and when, as the months went on, Anton became tired and ill, it was to affect everyone in the community. Having worn out his body and exhausted his mind, he looked for spiritual aid. He became moody and discouraged, and with my own exhaustion I was of little help to him. Despite the increasing pressures and lack of financial support, he bulldozed on; it was not in his nature to give up, he believed in being positive and not negative. Therefore when things looked bad he would push on in faith, 'relying on small miracles' as he called it! I admired his faith, but disapproved of its impracticability, which was to lead Simon into eventual curtailment.

Simon, still a babe-in-arms, had grown too rapidly and had tried to run before it could walk; we ran out of money and came into debt. At the same time Anton became ill and had to have a rest; it was fantastic that he had endured the two-and-a-half years at such a pace without a break. On his return he arrived at the office looking very grim, and I never saw him so ruthless as I did that evening when he announced that four of the houses and the office were to be closed, including the much needed Simonlight. The thought of throwing out all these men who needed us broke my heart into shreds as it must have done his. It was a brave action on Anton's part if it was necessary, but I could not condone it. It was as if we had given life to these boys and now were snatching it away from them. The time had come to leave Simon and Anton.

I walked miles in utter misery, not knowing where I was going, and not caring; my heart was torn apart and ached for the many lads who would have to suffer because of this curtailment. I felt as rejected as they would do when they found themselves back on the streets, homeless. It seemed so unfair, I felt, and unnecessary. I walked and walked and walked until I dropped; and when I woke up, I was in that mental hospital.

When I left the hospital a week later, with my haversack on my back, determined to begin again and learn from my mistakes, I had no idea where I was going to go or what I was going to do with myself. From Epsom I walked to London, trying to sort out my thoughts. Somehow I could not bring myself to go home, not as a failure. I had too much pride to face my highly successful father; it was against all my principles to go and sponge off friends and I did not want to answer questions anyway. Eventually I went to a friend of a friend, whom I hardly knew, and she very kindly put me up till I had sorted myself out.

I knew the best action I could take was to find a job and some digs. But my heart had always ruled my head and I knew my place was with the down-and-outs, so back I went to the bomb-sites in the East End. I was given the welcome of my life, they were so glad to see me. I did a 'skipper' that night with them. It was the first of many, and one I will never forget because it was the night that I decided to dig to the root of the problem of meths drinkers. They had all gone to sleep and I was keeping the wood fire going, sitting on an old milk crate. I was mentally reminiscing, going over the facts and figures of all the case histories I knew. Nearly every problem went back to childhood or to the war. It went back to when they were on alcohol or drugs; and then I remembered passing through Trafalgar Square a few days before and seeing debauched young, desperately young faces, who had the same haunted look in their eyes. I cogitated quietly.

"What yer thinkin'?" a voice asked. It was one of the lads.

"Hi! I didn't know you were awake. I was just thinking that meths drinkers are an advanced version of alcoholics and junkies."

"Yeah, that about sums us up."

"So really, to prevent the problem, one has to catch the kids?"

"Yeah, the teenagers are the ones, if yer lookin' for the prevention rather than cure."

"Those kids in Trafalgar Square?"

"Yup, anywhere in the West End yer'll find 'em."

"I might go down there some time and take a sniff."

"Yer'll do well; all yer have to do is become a beatnik."

"Become a beatnik?"

"Yeah, yer could do it."

"That's an idea."

"Well, I'm going to kip."

"Good night."

"Good night, luv."

CHAPTER FIVE

"WILL you come to bed with me tonight?" a pouting faced youth with blond shoulder-length hair asked me. His eyes were lethargic and looked as if they had just been sprinkled with tomato ketchup. His speech was slow and indifferent.

"No thank you," I answered. He screwed up his nose in disgust and wandered aimlessly away. I leant against the bar and watched Mother Hubbard con her second pint of beer off another long-haired youth. Her own hair was like straw, and the colour of her nicotined fingers. Her weather-beaten face was stamped with age and exposure. From her pocket she drew a soiled rag and wiped the froth from her lips before straightening her crushed felt hat and hitching up the petticoat that hung equally soiled, below a tatty brown dress. Mother Hubbard had nothing but what she was standing up in or what she could con out of the junkies surrounding her. Drugs or drink opened up the highway to hopelessness for her, as for everyone in the vicinity. Despite the notices behind the bar that anyone seen peddling drugs would be reported to the police, both pills and hash were being bargained for. Listless, thin-armed youths shuffled around; similar seedy specimens of the human race shambled in, their faces puffed with drugged slumber. Beneath ragged beards and swollen lips, haunted ghosts-like faces flinched in the agony of rage and shame. With shaking hands they tried to light their cigarettes. I held a steady match up for them and they looked at it in a kind of dull amazement. Night after night, day after day, week after week, month after month, they staggered groggily in having just had their evening fixes. This was their black cul-de-sac, a place where they accepted they would walk for evermore.

"Hi, man, what's your trouble? Not got a derry for tonight?" an underfed and overdosed frail youth asked me.

"Oh, I'm okay tonight a friend's putting me up. What about you?"

"I'm all right, man; I've been kipping down in the sewers under Piccadilly these past months. Sharing it with five of my mates."

"Comfortable?"

"Can't complain, really. Surroundings a bit crude mind you."

I hoped he was going to expand on his unusual living quarters, but old Mother Hubbard interrupted; she pointed to her empty glass and I shrugged my shoulders sympathetically. "No dole?" she whispered expectantly. I shook my head. "Oh!" she sighed, "Yer ain't got no money either. Not even enough fer another drink?" I shook my head again. "Oh!" was all she replied. She moved across to a group of youths standing by the juke box. A few minutes later she had returned with some silver and bought her third pint of brown ale. I noted she left nearly half of it in the bottle thus only half filling her own glass. I was wondering at this when she pushed the bottle towards me. "Ere, 'ave this," she said. This, I was to learn, was the most wonderful characteristic in all down-and-outs. Amongst their own kind, share and share alike. I was very touched, not to say conscience-ridden as I clutched the pound note in my pocket.

When I first rolled up in my denim jeans and polo-neck sweater beneath a matching denim shirt, with long straight hair hanging limply over my shoulders plus the traditional 'eye-concealing' fringe, I was no different from numerous other females there—or males! What with both sexes wearing elaborate rings and bracelets it only provided further complications in discriminating one from the other, though as often as not the men wore ear-rings in the form of crucifixes whilst the girls just had gold rings.

At first conversation was non-existent, and for over two weeks I spent every evening there without a word passing my lips, whilst conspicuous glances passed among them. Yet it was obvious that I was receiving the same treatment that every unknown face was given: a greeting of hostility in case I might be a social worker or some kind of religious preacher who might attempt to 'guide' or 'help' them. I discovered they were averse to any kind of patronising and equally reluctant to committing themselves to friendship. I found that as long as I was undemanding, they were prepared to give me a chance and talk to me. At the same time, having skirted various cafés and their dingy havens, I realised that fear of launching out into an unknown relationship or of rebuffal played a predominant part in their hostility. For months I patronised the addicts' hideouts and was given the cold shoulder; if I spoke without having been spoken to first, they turned their backs and walked away. It was made perfectly clear that I was not one of them. When I passed a group of youths talking they would fall silent until I was well out of ear-shot. If one of them was trying to con a drink out of someone, they never tried me. I was out on a limb and was made to feel so. This Coventry applied by all the youngsters was very hurtful, and often when I was out of sight I would burst into tears and pray for the guts and perseverance to return the following evening. It was not easy and I dreaded the slow, uncommunicative passing of time.

It was Doc Livingstone, universally so called by the beats because of his roamings, who broke the barrier. But he censored me for a week before deciding to accept me. He was a small, skinny man with a long face covered by a thin beard and side whiskers. He permanently wore an old pair of trousers under tails with a decorated ribbon suspended round his neck and a silver medallion attached to it, with 'Doc Livingstone' inscribed on it. He regarded himself as an 'old class' of beat.

"Twizzle and I are the old type you know," he said, "very few of them around now. Sure we're unconventional and have rejected society; sure we do strange things and look odd and are scruffy, but we're no part of these new pseudo-beats. We haven't misbehaved in a public place and are always polite. We have to suffer the reputation of these new creeps. You know I came in this coffee bar last week and the manageress threw us out because she thought we were some of those that had messed her around a few days previous—just because we look like them, we're taken for them. Sure we've stolen food and things in our time, but not like these new beats who take what they can from anyone, rich or poor. When Twizzle and I were in Manchester we used to walk out to the outskirts where the wealthy live and pinch from them. After all, these businessmen must have trodden on other people's toes to get their position and money, so we just kind of tread on theirs by swiping the occasional bottle of milk. But we never took anything from those who couldn't afford to give. And everything we had we shared. Twizzle would give his last cig. to me, and when I met him in Nottingham he gave me his last two-shilling bit because I hadn't eaten for three days. And I did the same when he came to London, but these new beats have no code of living. The best conners survive, the others fall by the way-side. You know, a sixteen-year-old kid came to London last week with twenty quid in her pocket. I had a tanner and bought her some food 'cause I thought she'd need her money and I suggested she put it into the post office. She was going to do it the next morning, but when I found her later that night those bastards had conned every penny from her and pinched her hand-grip. No wonder crime is on the increase when innocent newcomers are toughened in this way. Twizzle and I are the old type of beat, unconventional and scruffy, but sincere and reliable." In time I found this to be almost true.

Having been initially accepted and identified as one of them, I decided to press my point further and so I hit the road. With my pack on my back and a couple of blankets I trudged down to Trafalgar Square where some would be either in the toilets giving themselves fixes or in the National Gallery where as long as they were quiet they could sit un-disturbed, though the attendants soon made a rule that no one could sit for more than twenty minutes at a time, so when the lads were moved from one room they just went and parked themselves in another. Some, if they had conned

64

enough money, would spend the day in coffee bars or news theatres where they were able to sleep. Charing Cross Station buffet was a popular meeting point, and very rarely did I put my head round the doors and not see a couple of beats I knew. On Sunday nights all the beats in the district flocked to a Mission behind Trafalgar Square which opened for them and dished out free food and tea. Some of the kids who turned up could not have been more than fifteen, probably having just run away from home and come down south to seek the bright lights of London. The majority of those over eighteen were on the run from Borstal or the police, or had just come out of prison. Each and every person had a reason for hiding up in this underworld of iniquity. Yet little was kept secret between themselves, in fact, many of their devious activities were a source of boasting.

I remember Pinkie once saying to me. "We're getting engaged after Christmas."

"Oh, well done, good for you. Who's the lucky chap?"

"Riki, she lives up over Holloway way." I glanced at her dead-serious face and wondered if I was being pulled as a sucker.

"Don't look so confused," she continued. "Didn't you know I'm a lesbian and so's Riki? We'll be married in the spring. Would you like to come?"

"Surely! But looking on the practical side, who would marry you both?"

"Oh, Vicar will, he marries all the beats." I was taken aback.

"Do you mean he would marry two girls? I don't believe it."

"Of course he will; he has done in the past."

"What parish does he come from?" I innocently asked. A great hoot of laughter from Pinkie told me I had said something stupid.

"Oh, don't be so naïve, love, he's only called Vicar because he does marry us; he's just one of the beats like you and me." I fell into dumbfounded silence. There seemed little point in saying it wasn't valid, because matrimony to beats was like a dog with his bone—having enjoyed it, it was buried, and occasionally dug up thereafter.

Once on the road, I was taught how to con money from people. The usual story was that I had found a kid crying and on asking him the trouble, he had told me he had spent all his money and hadn't enough to get home, so I had generously given him half-a-crown only to discover later it was my last one! Could they possibly help me out? When travelling on the buses, we would search our pockets only to find we had left the money behind! We would give false names and addresses. On tubes we never bought tickets and at our destination swore that we had embarked one station before so only ended up paying fourpence. Pick-pocketing was another trade I was taught. The 'dip', or 'buzzer' as he is known, is a craftsman in his own right, who often works with a gang. The 'stalls' jostle their victim or by mistake barge into him and thus knock his hat off; the victim bends down to pick it up leaving his hip pocket exposed to sensitive fingers. Another favourite is for a dip to board a bus, get half-way up and then apparently realise that he is on the wrong route. As he struggles down through the passengers following him, he is ideally placed for fingering through inside pockets. Cinemas, race meetings and football matches are good hunting grounds. Christmas shopping crowds prove lucrative also! And armloads of parcels means good opportunities for shoving and hustling.

Peddling drugs discreetly is often carried out in a crowd. Often the peddlers work in pairs, like a young twenty-year-old boy I knew, who, with his girl-friend, hung around Waterloo Station. He was the peddler and the addicts approached him, but as they left the station they would bump into his girl-friend at the other end. She was the carrier, so that should he be picked up he would be as clean as a whistle.

One evening a youth took me back to his 'pad' which he was sharing with two other boys and three girls. We entered a room which was bare save for three mattresses, a gas ring and four syringes. They all sat there holding each other's

66

hands and as the evening progressed and the fixes began to wear off, they fell upon each other kissing and fondling the other's body; the sexual orgy that followed sickened me. Some drugs stimulate the sexual organs, and then it can be extra dangerous if not fatal, as on one occasion when I paid an unscheduled call upon Trix.

Trix had been a heroin addict for five years and was registered as such. She lived in a room in Hackney, though she spent most of her time in the West End. I climbed the concrete staircase and walked into her room without knocking, thinking she would be out with Bill. In the dim light I caught sight of Trix sitting on an upturned packing case. The room had an air of musty, stodgy decorum. Curtains of machine lace hung, dust-coloured, over a broken window. There was a foul odour, a vague mixture of alcohol and stale flesh. As I entered, a young Negress in her underclothes, sullenly smoking a cigarette, disappeared into the opposite room. Trix, hunched on the packing-case, had not heard my entrance for she was still busy with her hands. I trod warily across the rough planks, crudely laid. From the nails in the crumbling walls hung bits of desiccated photographs. I heard a car outside change gear as it passed. Suddenly Trix looked up, and for an instant we stared eye to eye. Under the faded electric light bulb something glowed in her hands. She sat motionless, her mouth a little open. Blood was trickling from her wrist. Between her long fingers was a piece of glass. I sprang forward, plucking at her. She surged to her feet, flinging her arms backwards for balance. Head down, my body arched, I went for her. She reeled backwards, thrusting out her hand with the piece of glass. I caught her bloody wrist. She struggled and flicked the glass towards my eyes. I ducked, but not far enough. I thudded against the wall as she hit me on the cheek. It made a dry, flat sound. She stumbled backwards, wailing, and jerkingly staggered out of the room towards the stairs. Blood from the gashes in my forehead crossed my field of vision as I sat rigid opposite the open door. With the palm of my hand I wiped the blood aside for a second before the stream continued. I spun downstairs after her. As I whirled out of the hallway, I saw her leaping at me with a brick. I lurched twisting in the air, grabbing the glass from her. I felt it strike me solidly on the temple. I rocked sideways trying to regain my balance but my head was spinning and the floor was rising. I saw her legs running into space before I hit the floor unconscious.

After a brief spell in hospital I went back to see Trix. She was giving herself a fix in the arm where the telling gash was healing. The veins down her arm were burnt out and now lay mauve and rotted. She greeted me cordially, and only when the evening was nearly over did she mention our fight. "Sorry abaht that do the other night. I'd 'a' been all right if Bill'd been here."

"Well, I have no desire to go through that a second time, so don't let's have any repercussions, okay?'

"Okay, man! Don't go on. It were just a feelin' I had at the time."

I realised the reason for that feeling was the absence of Bill, and quite suddenly it came to me that the simple failure of people to make contact with one another was often the cause of such human problems. What a paradox! We can bounce messages off the moon and send space probes to Mars, yet we are finding it more difficult as each day passes to communicate with the minds and hearts of those we love. Love is the climate in which all living things flourish. This language of love is designed to crack the shell of isolation by effective channels of communication. It is a universal language that is sadly neglected. Love is like gratitude, not much good unless you can show it. No doubt these addicts had relations who nominally loved them, but for these lone wolves it must be a tender understanding and a personal care, not just verbal concern. They needed compassion, not condemnation.

I was able to give compassion, not pity, and because of this giving it became a reciprocal action. They loved me in return. They began to love me so much that they asked me to fix them. At first I refused because I did not want to be part of it, I did not want to be involved. But I was involved and I was part of it. I was identified as one of them. So gritting my teeth so that I should not be sick, I began to give fixes. I had been fixing Stuart, a registered addict, for some weeks with ten grains, when it occurred to me that I might try cutting it down without him knowing. Over a period of three months I had cut him down to five grains without him noticing. I hoped there would be a time that I would be just injecting water into him. But as I learnt to deal with these drug addicts and look after them, I arrived at the opinion that a true addict is unable to come off without hospitalisation. Many a time a youth has wept his heart out on my shoulder because he is unable to give it up without a drug to take its place. Yet the majority who are fortunate enough to receive hospitalisation return straight to drugs on their release. Therefore there are two actions necessary to help the addicts and control addiction. The addicted must receive medical aid, and the source must be stopped. Until the peddlers are exterminated, drug addiction will be on the up-and-up not only amongst the young, but amongst all ages and classes. I don't blame the young for their idiocy, I blame the hard, calculating peddler who provides the ammunition for them to destroy themselves with—and they do.

CHAPTER SIX

DARKNESS had fallen and the steady rain had changed to a mere drizzle. Black shadows frowned over the deserted streets as tattered clouds were driven in scattered formation across the sky. My clothes hung coldly to my back. I walked faster across the slumbering City. The chill wind was freezing my face and numbing my fingers. I passed an old nightwatchman, sitting solemnly in his canvas box, staring at the glow of the brazier and the line of red lights that surrounded the road works. I called a cheerful greeting as I passed, which he acknowledged with a grunt. I crossed the vast empty bus terminus, my steps amplified in the eerie silence. Deserted buses stood in neat rows, their windows glazed and reflective. I continued down drenched streets where rivulets scuttled down steps and whirlpools gushed round gratings. Past grey uniform buildings and a grave-yard where the rain pattered mournfully upon the tombs— upon the just and unjust alike. Everywhere was filled with the raw night air, damp, dark and cold.

I came to a junction and turned left, leaving the White-chapel Road behind me. I wondered if they would be here. The wet breeze blew my hair over my face in a kind of mockery. I was nearly there. Just past these abandoned derelict buildings, carcasses of 'home', and beyond that creeping wall. The stillness spread like a blanket into the distance. I approached the ramp as softly as I could, and advanced from behind the sodden wall. There was a dull red glow of a wood fire. Beside it cowered figures with hands outstretched to meet the grateful warmth. With limbs hud-dled together and heads bowed, they bent over the fitful light. In the smouldering embers these stricken figures sat the nights out, amongst the ashes and dust and debris of the bomb-site. The figures neither spoke nor turned to look at me. Quietly I moved across to one of the stooping figures who clasped a bottle; gently I unlocked his fingers and the glass smashed to pieces as it hit the ground, echoing across the night. The stooping figure rocked forward and I grabbed him as he was about to fall into the embers. His clothes were soaked. Little by little, with an intense effort, he lifted his head and looked at me. His eyes were red and glazed.

"Hello, Benghazi! It's all right, it's only me. How are you?"

He stared expressionlessly at my face. His lips began to move, but no sound came from them in reply. I dug into my pockets and produced a packet of squashed cigarettes. I lit one for him and placed it between his swollen lips. I looked around to see how many of the regulars were here tonight. I counted eleven heads in all, that was including the three prostrate bodies lying over by the wall. I recognised seven faces by name. Some had lived on this bomb-site for seventeen years, some were newcomers. Others who had once lived here had passed away, their guts and stomach burnt dry by methylated spirits or eau-de-cologne. Some just died of exposure; a few so drunk, fell into the fire and were burnt to death, and the occasional one was killed by some angry drunkard. They lived animals' lives with a law of their own. How I longed for a lighter room, bright fires and cheerful faces, the music of happy voices, words of love and welcome and warm hearts. It was a night to be home, asleep by a warm hearth.

I glanced across at the heaped bodies of Canada, Hank, Steela Horse, Jock and Paddy. Their faces, concealed behind knotted stubble and stale old grime, were muffled under flea-ridden overcoats. Benghazi suddenly rocked forward again and I put out a supportive hand. He seemed to pull himself to consciousness as he felt my grip and smiled at me in recognition, revealing a few discoloured fangs scattered around in his mouth. He gave me his hand in friendship. It was rough and very dirty, his gritty fingernails were jagged and yellow. He was unwholesome and animal-like. Each night I met him he seemed to grow weaker and more feeble and care-worn. The mask of death that I had seen so many times before, was about to claim another victim.

Canada turned over and stretched out for a bottle beside him.

"It's empty, Canada. You're wasting your time," I told him. He fixed his eyes on me, eyes that were drunk and strained. With trembling hands he picked the bottle up and put it to his lips, then threw it down with disgust. A look of persecution crossed his face. I went over to him and sat myself down on an old petrol tin that someone had once drunk out of. Benghazi watched my movements like a devoted dog.

"How are things?" I asked gently.

Canada scratched his wiry hair infested with lice, and fixed his eyes once again on me. "Ow, Sal. Wheeeel. Vrrry wheeeel." I gave him a cigarette.

Jock, having heard voices, came to. " 'Ello, Sal," he greeted me and put his hand out for a cigarette. I threw him one.

"You dry tonight, Jock?" I tried to hide my surprise.

"Ay. Ain't got much option. Came out of nick this morning."

"I thought I hadn't seen you around lately. Actually I heard you'd joined another school of meths drinkers down by the Elephant and Castle."

"Ay, and we all got picked up by the cops. They gave me a month."

"And what's the score now, or shouldn't I ask?"

"Ahrr! Dunno. Try and stay dry, I suppose. Git m'self a job tomorrow. Try Covent Garden in the morning—or Spitalfields."

"Well, good luck." I knew that if I probed further he would clam up. "A few new faces round here tonight. Who's that bloke?"

"That's Gypsy Bill. Used to be a cell mate of mine. We've done time together, like. 'E's a good enough bloke, a bit keen on using 'is fists, mind. 'E's a good friend," he repeated thoughtfully.

Canada turned to Jock and waved a trembling hand.

"Passsh de botttttle," he rolled out in his drunken, stinking stupor.

"No, laddie, this one's empty. Try Benghazi. 'E 'ad some."

I butted in. "No, he hasn't. I had a look earlier."

Jock stumbled to his feet and bent over Steela Horse. He kicked him awake. "Horse! Horse! Canada wants some jake." There was a muffled grunt of agreement; Jock took the bottle that he was clasping tightly to his chest, and handed it to the tottering Canada. "Sit down b'fore yer fall down," Jock cried and pushed him over. He crashed on top of Benghazi and the two of them rolled in the mud, grappling for the bottle.

Meanwhile Paddy was whimpering by the almost dead fire. I was about to get up and see what the matter was when Jock put a restraining hand on me. "Ye canna do anythin' for 'im, Sal. 'E won't last the night out, I don't think." I looked at the writhing body, the haggard face looking mauve in the spark-light of the embers. The eyes were sunken and black and the open mouth gasping for breath. Bile dribbled down his chin. I had seen it all before. I closed my eyes and prayed. I forced myself to my feet and went and knelt beside him. I took his ice-cold languid hand and rubbed it. For a second he opened his puffed eyes and gave me a glassy stare. I smiled caringly at him. I knew there was nothing I could do, I knew that he was beyond medical help. I smiled again and grasped his hand. As long as he knows he's not alone, that someone cares, that was all I wanted to transmit to him in my smile. It was so little and cost me nothing, and yet could mean the whole world to a dying man.

A few hours later, everyone had drifted back to sleep. The fire and Paddy had died together. I looked around at his mates; many of them would be joining him soon, and they did not care. They had nothing left in life to live for. They had hit 'rock bottom'. For them, time was timeless; only the bottle counted. Methylated spirits was their passport to oblivion—finally their passport to death. How can they sleep, I thought, Paddy was one of them. But they were used to it. I remember Canada telling me one day when he was dry that during the cold winter of 1963 the police were picking up six dead men a week off the bomb-sites. I felt the chill run down my spine. I felt so small, so inadequate. I blamed myself, I blamed society, I blamed the world. Whose fault was it that these men were forsaken? Fellow-mankind. Let moralists and philosophers say what they like, but it is questionable that a guilty person could have suffered such misery as I did that night, being innocent. I wept tears, not for Paddy, for he had been released from his torture, not for his pathetic animal-like buddies, but for me and my family and friends; that we regarded ourselves as Christians and yet allowed a man, a young man at that, to pass away unnoticed. Here today and gone tomorrow, who cared? No one. I sat, alone, penitent. The rain seemed to pour down more hopelessly and more heavily than ever. The puddles became deeper and dirtier. The men, in their mighty ocean of solitude, slept on. Time itself seemed to have grown dull and old, as if day was unable to displace the melancholy night. I began to shiver with cold, it was so wet.

Stiffly I rose from beside Paddy and went in search of wood to re-start the fire. I combed the surrounding bomb-sites, but it was all too damp. When I returned to the ramp, Jock was awake.

"So Paddy never made it," he sighed.

"No, you were right. What should we do with him?"

"In the morning, ye'd better go to the police station and report it. They'll deal with the body, they're used to it."

"Will he get a burial?" I asked.

"Only if someone'll cough up to pay." He got to his feet. "God! I'm bloody well soaked through. I'm not stayin' here any longer." He stepped over Canada and Benghazi, smashing the bottle as he went.

"Where are you going?" I called after him.

"Plenty of derries round here with warm fires, d'ye no' ken them?"

"I know the one in Fairfax Street, where Big Michael hangs out."

"Och! there's a nearer one than that. Come along and see for yourself." I glanced at my human derelicts lying in the mud; when dawn came they would be out scavenging the gutters for their breakfast.

"Comin', lassie?" Jock called back at me. I left them to the approaching dawn and followed him.

Back on the road, lorries with their loads began to rattle past, and the first commuters slunk out of their houses. Exhausted with discomfort and sick from exposure, the crude spirit drinkers and the ordinary dossers lay amongst the thrown-out debris, glaring at the intruders, cursing at their life and their world. Beyond the sunrise, people were truly living; living and not existing from day to day, from hour to hour with questions of how to fill their bellies, how to keep warm, how to live. Whilst they squatted amongst rubble, empty bottles and trodden cigarette butts, watching the world dispassionately, trying to divert their minds from the crucifixion of living.

"What's the matter? Has Paddy's death upset ye?" Jock was saying.

"No, Jock, just thinking. A mistake, I know, so don't say it."

"Noo, I wouldna'. D' ye know Bignall Street at all?"

"It's off Cannon Street isn't it?"

"Ay. There's a wee derry there that'll give us shelter for the night, what little there is left." We came to another bomb-site and clambered over a wall and made our way through the rubble towards a row of houses on the far side. We found a gap in the fence that surrounded the buildings and climbed over falling stone. One of the houses was roofless, and one side of the wall had collapsed. We came to the third dilapidated ruin and entered it through a gap in the wall where once had stood a door. "Careful!" Jock warned, pointing to a missing step in the cop-ridden stair-case. My eyes were growing accustomed to the dark, but it was the smell that made me want to turn tail; it was sweet and sickly and desperately strong. I stopped on the decaying landing and leaned against the wall. The smell was everywhere.

"What's the matter?" Jock called as he ascended the second staircase. "No feelin' too good?"

"I'm all right, Jock. It's just that ghastly smell."

"Och! that's meths. The lads are up here. Come and meet them."

I climbed after him, passing a large hole in the wall where the wind and rain were driving in. Suddenly I heard the quiet murmur of voices. As I entered the room a bright fire leapt cheerfully in the hearth, making friendly shadows on the wall. In the corner was an iron bed on which lay three cramped figures. Before the fire sat another three on the dusty floor, their twisted faces grinning in welcome. The rest of the room was empty; it was dark and murky, full of dust and rust and rotting with wood-worm. Someone handed me a bottle, the stink became unbearable. I thought I was going to be sick. Speechless, grinding my teeth for self-control, I handed it back to greedy hands. "Sit down, Sal. Ye'll feel better if yer get some kip," Jock urged. I joined him on the floor by the fire. " 'Ere, have my donkey jacket for yer head." He put it down as a pillow for me to use. I was grateful for it. I lay listening to the drunken wanderings of the men as they passed the bottle round. It was difficult to distinguish what they were actually saying, but as far as I could gather they were talking about the war. This, I was to discover, was the predominant topic of conversation amongst the meths drinkers because that was the last time they felt they had been real men.

I must have dozed off, for when I came round the three figures that had been on the bed had gone. "Kip well?" Jock asked as he put more wood on the fire.

"Yes, thanks, I must have been tired. Where is everyone?"

"Och! they've gone off to work."

"But would they get a job in that condition? Surely not?"

"They weren't on meths, you know. They were just dossers without any place to go and no money for a bed and breakfast."

"If they work, they must have some money, come off it!" I replied.

"Ay, they get a wage, but they spend it in the pub during the evening."

"What, the whole lot? Anyway, what kind of work do they do?"

"Casual labour; paid by the hour so it don't make no difference to the employer if they don't turn up ever again. Mostly they try the caterin' firms, or the younger ones try the building sites or Covent Garden."

"And how do these blokes get their money?" I pointed to the three unconscious bodies on the floor.

"Pinch it, or con it. Or a few of them stagger into a hardware store and demand a bottle of meths. The chap's only too pleased to give it to them—it's cheaper than having your shop smashed to pieces, and they can do a lot of damage before the police arrive."

"Personally I'm surprised the police don't arrest them from the ramp."

"Och, they don't want us infesting up their cells, spewing everywhere. Ye see, we're more trouble than we're worth, really. As long as they know where to put their finger on us any time they want, they're happy to let us go."

"But couldn't you get help from the Welfare State like other people?"

"Don't be daft, lassie."

I tried to visualise hundreds of Benghazis pouring into the local authority centre, bringing with them the stench of dirt and surrounded by the peculiar and nauseating aura created by poverty, crime and self-destructive compulsions. Would I, too, see them as inferior and representing merely a job of work of the least inspiring and most exacting kind? Would I shout at them and drive them into a pattern which would make that job as easy as possible? Would I despise them and resent them as a blot on my life and society, and a waste of time, effort and money? Would I make them the unhappy products of the cruelty, ignorance and regimentation of these so-called places of refuge?

"You see, Sal," one of them told me once, "we're unclean. No one wants to touch us. Sure, we get given advice and occasionally help in order to try and break the vicious circle we're in, but you should see the non-existent conviction with which they offer it! It's like putting a penny in the slot machine and we're expected to play the tune. We try, but Rome wasn't built in a day. You can't take us out of one environment and dump us in another, expecting us to fall in with your standards and ways of living. It all takes time and patience, and no one in this day and age has either."

"Well lassie, I'll be off to find myself a job. What are ye goin' to do? Ye can stay here if ye want, they'll no worry ye." Jock rose and dusted down his ragged trousers.

"No, I'll be pushing on, thanks, Jock."

"Will ye be back tonight on the ramp?"

"Maybe. I'm not quite sure what the day holds for me yet. Anyway, I'll be around, so I'll see you. Good luck with the job."

We shook hands and went our different ways. The rain had stopped, and the tradesmen's doors were open. Smoke rose from the chimneys, and traffic rumbled by. I walked towards the City in solitary meditation. What was the answer to this problem? Obviously the authorities did not have the right approach, and only created resentment. The answer must lie in making the men believe in themselves. Without faith in themselves, and without having somebody who truly cares whether they live or die, how can they be expected to rise above this depression? Was it not possible for one to say, I love this man, and by doing so, rekindle in him a sense of his own dignity and a love in himself, that he might regain his self-respect? Love, respect, call it what you will, was the vital spark which was missing from these broken personalities who sought shelter. There were thousands of such men now; tomorrow there might be millions. They did not advertise their presence, but they were there, waiting to be released from the torture of living. They were people who had failed to find a proper place in our society and who rejected all our standards, perhaps through misfortune or perhaps through choice. The majority, though, were afflicted with some difficulty or inadequacy of personality which contributed to this destitution. I felt sure the only answer was in love.

I turned into the police station to report the death of an unknown citizen of the name of Paddy. *Love*—take away love and there was no more life.

CHAPTER SEVEN

I BEGAN to devote my days to mixing with the beats and my nights to the dossers and crude spirit drinkers. I bummed around with my grotty long-haired friends around Trafalgar Square. If we had conned enough money we would sit in Lyons with a cup of tea which we would pass between us drawing out the time as much as possible until we were thrown out. On to the National Gallery, where we would sit and doze till we were asked to leave, and so to the Square post office where we would lounge around on the ground, having scanned it for dog-ends. Eventually the police would be called in and once again we would be moved on, so across to Charing Cross Station where we would con a few shillings and cigarettes and return to another Lyons. This was the cycle of the day till the pubs opened.

I became bored and frustrated. I had successfully identified myself with the beats, but had now come to a dead end. I was being of no practical help apart from assisting with the occasional fix. In contrast, my nights were too short for all the work I had to fit in. With money I conned during the day I bought loaves of bread and cheese and cigarettes to take round to my dossers in the evening. When the pubs closed at eleven and the beats dispersed to derries or night clubs or just to walk the road till morning, I collected from Charing Cross left luggage department the food I had bought previously. I moved into the waiting-room where I began to butter the bread and fill the sandwiches. Onlookers watched me with disbelief. This task completed, I went down to a tea stall on the Embankment where long-distance lorry-drivers stopped during the night to freshen up. Here I bought eight cups of tea and instead of drinking them poured them into a Thermos flask which I carried (in time I got to know the Italian gentleman behind the stall, and filling my flask with free tea became his contribution towards my work).

About midnight I commenced my rounds. Waterloo Station, Elephant and Castle, back along the Embankment where dossers slept on the benches, down the alleyways of Fleet Street where they would huddle in doorways, a brisk walk across the deserted City to Stepney. I had usually finished by five, and after a quick kip I was back in Trafalgar Square at eleven, conning unsuspecting sightseers.

Initially I had offered the beats, like the dossers, an un-critical, undemanding and tolerant attitude and a readiness to understand their problems. With the dossers I had proved it was possible to progress to more demanding relationships and towards more positive goals. In contrast, when deal-ing with the beats there was a hard core of resistance which I seemed unable to break through. Certainly I had fulfilled a role as one of them, but despite all the tolerance and un-derstanding I gave, I was unable to penetrate their tough shells. I was an intellectual beat in their eyes, and was accordingly treated with greater respect and eventually labelled 'Sally the Christian'. Anyone else tagged as this was automatically despised and spat upon yet they accepted me and admired me for it. But obviously not enough to fol-low my example. Yet this was not entirely true, as time proved.

I met Twizzle and Brazil Nut in the post office. French Jean and American Charlie were sitting with them; from their heavy eyelids and dilated pupils I gathered they had just had a fix.

"Seen Doc Livingstone? He's missing. No one's seen him since he took sixteen people out to Stanmore to a party." Twizzle said.

"He's probably stoned, man; he'll be okay," I replied.

"No, man; there weren't no party there. He did it as a joke."

"Well, they've probably killed him then. I would have, if he'd done that to me," I assured him, but Twizzle still looked unhappy.

"I think he's been nicked. He would have been back by now, otherwise."

The low, drugged drawl of American Charlie interrupted. "I'm goin' to the Duke. Comin'?"

We went. En route we conned some money, though Brazil Nut had plenty—her crazy mixed-up father sends her fifty pounds every month to pay for her to have English lessons. The beats spend it for her on alcohol and drugs. Halfway through the evening Twizzle, French Jean and myself ran out of cash, so we left the pub and wandered into Soho. "We'll get more if we split up. Sally, you cover Greek Street, and Frenchie, you do Wardour Street, I'll do Dean Street. Meet you back here in fifteen minutes," Twizzle instructed. "Try the spades and the Chinese blokes, Sally; they're easier meat and usually quite generous. See yer." The tall, lank figure of Twizzle loped off in the direction of Dean Street, whilst French Jean, with his shoulders hunched, limped grotesquely for effect, towards Wardour Street.

On the corner of Greek Street, I pretended to look at the cinema advertisements; from experience I knew that I would be approached without having to attract anyone's attention. A young Indian brushed past me, his hand knocking me slightly. I felt repulsed, but forcing a friendly smile I turned to him.

"You come with me," he said, highly delighted with his catch.

"Very kind of you, but I must make a telephone call. You couldn't lend me a tanner?" I enquired. He began to delve into his pocket.

"You come with me after telephone call?" He produced the sixpence.

"Well, no, I won't if you don't mind." I put my hand out for the money.

"You no come with me, you get no sixpence." Angrily he stumped away. Quietly to myself I let out a string of abuse.

Two other similar conditioned offers were made before a West Indian spade tossed me a shilling on request. I extracted four cigarettes from a sympathetic Malayan boy and a Bounty Bar to eat from a sailor. Six football supporters wrapped in red and white scarves and bobble hats and con-responding rosettes gaily sauntered towards me. "You couldn't help me out with a shilling for some breakfast tomorrow morning?" I asked.

One of them turned to his friends. "Now lads, here we have a damsel in distress. Unless you give her some money she'll have to go without her breakfast tomorrow."

A red-faced man, matching the red stripes of his scarf replied, "Well, lassie, what can you do for it? Sing, dance perhaps?"

I felt myself turn the same colour. "I've got no voice."

"Gentlemen, I beg you for mercy," one of them cried out. "Into your pockets and see what fruits you have." Everyone emptied their pockets.

The first speaker took over. "Two pennies each towards this most excellent cause." He took off his bobble cap and everyone threw their money in.

"Thank you gentlemen, I will remember you as I scoff bacon and eggs tomorrow."

"A delightful idea, fair maiden." The first speaker bent low and kissed my hand. "Adios amigos." With merry laughter they continued down the road.

Fifteen minutes later the three of us met and were pooling our gains. Between us we had conned fourteen shillings and fivepence. "I'm hungry; what about some fish and chips?" French Jean suggested. As we were ambling round Soho, our hands sticky with vinegar and grease, we were discussing where we were going to sleep the night.

"I slept in the Alphabet last night," Twizzle was saying.

"Bit noisy wasn't it?" I remarked, remembering that when I was there the juke box never stopped till closing time at seven in the morning.

"Yeah, yer get used to it. I slept right through last night, never heard a sound."

"Last time I tried it, people kept walking over me," French Jean said.

"Yeah, well whadderyer expect when yer sleep on the dance floor? I go and park myself on the platform where the juke box is; yer less likely to be kicked there. Anyway that's where I'm kipping tonight; at least it's warm," Twizzle confirmed.

"I'll come," Frenchie replied, "You'll have to give me five bob to get in, otherwise I'll have to con it. Where're you kipping, Sally?"

"I'm not, at least not yet. I've got some work to do." They stood still and gazed at me in horror.

"Work? What do yer do a crazy thing like that for?"

"Not what you mean by work, I don't get paid for it. It's voluntary. I go round the dossers and meths drinkers and give them food."

'You must be mad,' they cried simultaneously. I made no comment.

"Yer scatty, man." Conversation waned and then, "Whadderyer do it for?"

"Because they're people like us with no money, no food and no home, and many of them are too old, too ill or are too disabled to help themselves. You're all right, Twizzle, you're comparatively young and agile and able to look after yourself. The public are fairly tolerant towards your conning them and the aimless way you all bum around. They make excuses for your youth and immaturity that they won't make for the old dirty dossers."

"But yer said yerself, they're so dirty an' horrible."

"Give yourself twenty years, Twizzle, and you'll be one of them." He lapsed into silence. He had nothing to say for himself. We walked on.

Frenchie broke the silence: "Whereabouts do you meet them?"

"They're all over London, but time being limited I usually concentrate on the East End and Waterloo Station area."

"Whadderyer actually do for 'em?" Twizzle asked, forgetting his sulks.

"Well, I take them food and cigarettes and hot tea. Occasionally I get given the odd piece of clothing for them which I take along. But more important to them is a friendly smile which does not cost me a penny." I withheld myself from adding that it would not cost them anything either.

"I dunno why yer want to bother yerself with 'em," Twizzle commented.

"Perhaps because no one else is prepared to; I've always been a supporter of lost causes," I mused. "I'm a sentimentalist."

"Yer just daft. Yer wastin' yer money. They don't appreciate it."

"I'd rather spend it on that, which will keep them alive, than drugs and alcohol which will only lead to your own destruction." My two comrades had nothing to reply. "Well, I'm going to see if I can borrow a car for tonight. I'll see you tomorrow in the Square."

"Borrow? You mean take one. I'll do it for you if yer want."

"No. I do actually mean borrow. I have a friend who occasionally lends me one. It saves a lot of time and a lot of walking."

"Okay, man, see yer tomorrow." I was turning to leave them both when Twizzle called after me, "Hey, want any 'elp tonight?"

I could not believe my ears. Trying not to sound too eager I replied, "Twizzle, I could always do with help, however little."

He looked at Frenchie. Their eyes met. "Come on, Frenchie, wot abaht it?"

"No, what's the point of all three of us being mad," he replied.

"Just this once, Frenchie," Twizzle pleaded. I kept quiet, not wanting to appear to influence them either way. "Whassa matter? Yellow?"

"You accusing me of being yellow? Get lost, man."

"Prove it then. Come with us." Twizzle set the challenge.

"Okay, man, I'll come for the lark and show you I'm not yellow." It was settled. I promised to meet them at the Duke at ten-thirty after I had fetched the car.

As I drove to pick them up, I was so inflated with my own egoism that should I have had a halo I would not have fitted into the car. I felt I had broken through to them at last. I checked myself as my thoughts ran away with me on what future help they could give me. "Slow down, Sally, or you'll be pressurising them too much and all your good will be undone," I murmured to myself. I made a promise that after tonight I would never mention to them the possibility of helping me further. It must be their idea and come from within themselves. As I turned the corner to the Duke, I was disillusioned. There was no sign of Twizzle or Frenchie. I waited till the pub emptied at closing time, optimistically, but in vain. At midnight, with still no sign of them, I left for Waterloo Station.

"Hi, Sally, over 'ere," Twizzle called across to me next morning in the Square. " 'Ere, 'ave a drag?" He handed me a soggy cigarette. I was tired after a hectic night with my dossers. There had been a fight, and one of them had had his teeth knocked out and because he was bleeding so much I had escorted him to hospital and sat up half the night with him in Casualty.

"How are things, Twizzle?" On purpose I avoided discussing the previous night. "Did you sleep at the Alphabet after all?"

"Yea, with Frenchie and God. 'Ere Sal, sorry about last night. We went conning after yer left and forgot about time."

"Forget it, Twizzle, it didn't matter," I said as casually as I could, feeling my anger brewing up inside me.

"Tell yer what, man, we'll come another night. Okay?"

"Okay, I go every night. Just give the word," I said pointedly. Creeping Jesus arrived and the conversation switched to sex.

The next time I had offers of help was on Christmas Eve. There was a group of us on the steps of St. Martin's Church. A tramp shuffled by and waved to me. "Do you know him?" Doc Livingstone enquired.

"Yes, he has a derry over in Elephant and Castle that I visit."

"Yea, Twizzle was telling me about you looking after these dossers. I think it's a great idea. Jolly good luck to you, and if you ever want our help, of course, just let us know."

I drew a deep breath and took the plunge. "As a matter of fact, I need some support tomorrow night, if you're not doing anything. I've got four families cooking and baking food for me, but no one to help dish it out."

"Sure, we'll help. Lads," he said, turning to his group, "to-morrow evening we're going to help Sally give out Christmas dinners to the poor old boys on Waterloo Station. Where do you want us to meet?"

"I should think platform one at about nine-thirty. If you can bring any cigarettes without having to steal them, I'd be most grateful."

"Right, lassie, we'll see what we can do."

"Don't worry if you can't; I've bought a thousand," I added.

"Where did you get the money from for those?" Scouse asked.

"I've been working in the post office these past two weeks as a Christmas recruit. Sorting and delivering."

"So that you could buy food and cigarettes for your boys?" Doc was obviously impressed with my motives for working.

"Partly, and to buy presents for my family," I admitted. They looked at me as if I was an apparition. Doc spoke for them.

"I admire you, Sally. You're not one of these people that stand up on a soap-box saying what's it's like to have Christ in you and how easy it is to be saved. You don't go around calling yourself a Christian and the next minute sticking a knife in the other fellow's back, if you know what I mean, like these preaching bastards we sometimes have to listen to. I was staying with one a few weeks ago. He told me Christ was inside him, yet when he asked one of the lads to get some coal and he didn't, he swore abuses at him and told him he was an idle swine and a bad influence on the rest of us, and then he threw him out on to the street. Was that being a Christian?"

"It's not for me to say, Doc. All I know from my own experience, is that to be a practising Christian is the hardest lifelong task one can ever set oneself. And believe me no human being can help you; that's what makes it so difficult."

"Yer got quite a brain, ain't yer?" Sloppy Terrence contributed.

"I've learnt from bitter experience. Nothing else can teach you. As it comes from the Almighty above, it goes back to the Almighty above."

"You really do believe we are the instruments of God, don't you?" Doc said.

"Absolutely, Doc."

"I don't believe in all this religion," Scouse interrupted, crossly.

"Dear Scouse, this is nothing to do with religion. This is to do with believing in Christ and following His trail from Bethlehem to Calvary on the way that He lived and loved. It doesn't mean going to church, taking the sacraments, going to prayer meetings. It's far more simple than that, and a hundred times more difficult—being a Christian is simply being Christ-like."

"I wouldn't know anything about that."

"Don't worry, Scouse, I'm still suffering from birth pangs myself."

He got up and dusted down his jeans, and said "I'm off conning; see yer at Duke's tonight." The group seemed to split up, but Doc turned to me before leaving. "We'll be outside platform one tomorrow at nine-thirty, so don't you worry, lassie." We shook hands warmly. "Happy Christmas to you, Doc, and thanks."

I spent that Christmas Day driving from Bournemouth to Petersfield to Guildford to London, collecting the food I had been promised from the various scattered sources. Fortunately my mother had lent me her van for this food run, otherwise I would have been in dire trouble. By nine o'clock on Christmas night I had acquired over a hundred mince pies and home-made sausage rolls, cakes and sandwiches, biscuits and four giant-sized flasks of tea. My little van was crammed with goodies and exuding delicious smells as I drove into a trainless Waterloo Station. Parking the van, I walked to platform one where I was not only to meet the beats but also the Dobbie family, who were insistent upon giving up part of their own family festivities to come and help me.

I was fifteen minutes early, so I began to wander round the station seeing how many we would have to feed. I had reached the other end when I was startled to hear myself summoned over the loud-speaker to the station-master's office. I began to worry. What had happened now? The station-master was standing outside for me. "You Miss Sally Trench? Good, your boy-friend's on the other end of my telephone. Will you kindly make your conversation brief, I'm not a social Answerphone." I grabbed the receiver apologising profusely. "Hello, Sally here. Who's that?"

I recognised Doc's voice on the other end. "Me, Twizzle and company. Look, Sally, we're stuck out at Crystal Palace and we've just discovered there's no transport running and we can't get out to help you." I smiled to myself.

"Never mind, Doc, I'll manage. What are you doing out at Crystal Palace?"

"We're staying here with Brother Karl. Look, we really are very sorry. Truly we had ever intention of coming. You do believe me, don't you?"

"Yes, of course, Doc. Honestly it doesn't matter."

"No, well, I don't like letting you down, and I did say we would be there."

"Forget it, Doc, it's quite unimportant. Nothing's going to come to a stop because you can't make it. Anyway I have got some others coming."

"Well, Twizzle's just had an idea. If you've got the car, why not come and get us? We would love to help." I hesitated before replying.

"I don't think so, Doc. I'll be running round all night picking the dossers up to take them to a bomb-site where I'm organising a party. I don't think it's worth-while adding to the mileage by coming out to pick you up, and I would have to do two loads because I can only fit four in the van."

"Oh! All right then." He sounded disappointed. "Happy

Christmas to you, lassie, and I'm sorry to have let you down like this."

"Happy Christmas to you all, and don't think about it again."

"Okay, Scouse and Twizzle say Happy New Year."

I put the receiver down and turned to face a puzzled station-master.

"Did I hear you say you're organising a dosser's party tonight?"

"Yes, that's right. Like to come?" He laughed.

"That's very kind of you, Miss Trench, but I'm glad to have met you. I think it's a grand idea and it's nice to know that there's someone who cares what happens to these people." Jovially we shook hands and exchanged greetings. I returned to platform one to wait the arrival of the others.

Our Christmas party was a great success. Having fed those at Waterloo Station, we drove along the Embankment picking up the lonely figures who were straying into the Christmas night. In two loads we arrived at the party bomb-site. We filed out of the cars with boxes of food and gigantic flasks of piping hot tea. I left them there whilst I drove round to the meths cellars in search of more. I found them wrapped in old newspapers amongst the bottles and thrown out débris; they squatted together for warmth, trying to divert their minds from their misery. Over the road drifted the sound of gay music and corks popping. It was the time to sing, drink, dance and be merry.

"Hi! You look cold," I sympathised. They opened their eyes wearily. "If you like, I'll take you to a place where you can have some food and hot drinks." Again they opened their eyes; their faces were hollow and expressionless and I felt as if I was looking right through their eyes. They were living bodies, but dead souls.

The music from across the way broke into the Gay Gordons and the high pitched whoopees became louder. I bent down and one by one got them to their feet. "Trust me, and I'll bring you back here after if you like." I took one by the hand and led him to the car. The others followed.

As we drew up at the bomb-site a large fire was blazing. Silhouetted against the leaping flames were my unwanted friends. The Dobbies were passing the food round; the lads, sitting on upturned petrol cans and buckets, were talking and laughing. One of them, clasping a bottle of eau-de-cologne which he had been drinking, rose and gave a voluble welcome to the new arrivals; seats were found for them on dustbin lids. Mrs. Dobbie and I ladled out the tea while Colonel Dobbie was kept busy passing the sausage rolls and mince pies. Charles, the son, produced a trumpet and began to play 'Silent Night', and they began to sing. It was a wonderful sight. As the stars shone bright and midnight struck, voices that perhaps had not sung for ten years, accompanied the carol the trumpet blew. It did not go unheard for through the darkness their voices echoed across the Stepney bomb-sites and more figures appeared. Some Germans and Norwegians heard us from their mission-hostel a mile and a half away, and followed the music till they found us. They had been going to bed after the evening's celebrations when they heard us start up and just had to come and investigate. So they too joined in singing the carols in their native tongues. Smiles that I had never seen before on certain faces appeared. Cold, despairing eyes became filled with warmth and light. Haunted faces lost their creases and hunched shoulders straightened as they sang aloud, and laughed from the depths of their hearts. It was real and it was wonderful.

It must have been about three in the morning. It was all over. How I hated myself dropping them back at their respective spots to walk the night out, to become the 'unknown citizen' again. Around the fire we had shared a feeling, a feeling of belonging to one another, a feeling of need. It had brought us together as one family. Now I blamed myself for giving them to the cold night and a blanket of loneliness. At the time I knew I had no choice but to return them to their chasm of nonentity, yet now as I drove home to a warm bed I could not clear my conscience of the responsibility of picking them off the road and throwing them back on it. "God, why am I so powerless to help?" I whispered. His answer came seconds later as I fell asleep at the wheel. Fortunately the road was clear, and as the car swung across to the other side I woke with a start. I was only human, too.

CHAPTER EIGHT

On Boxing Day I visited Singer in the London Hospital. Singer was an old friend. I had known him nearly a year. We had first met on the ramp where he had sat with his mates brewing up 'jake', a mixture of lemonade and methylated spirits. Simon had just opened its night shelter in Cable Street, and we were out searching the ramp for customers. Singer was one of our first. They came back with us to our newly painted shelter where the inevitable Simon cup of tea awaited them. With Tommy McGeachy, Singer and Benghazi gathered almost nightly in our meths pit where they would doss down with their bottles on mattresses on the floor. When they woke in the morning they were welcomed upstairs for a hot meal. In our Simon shelter they could live without questions, pressures or money. Money for food was our big problem, but we managed to get round this by scavenging. Every morning we went to the Spitalfields fruit and vegetable market where we got on to our hands and knees and hunted for thrown-away scraps— bruised potatoes, battered turnips, broken stalks of rhubarb, lettuce and cabbage leaves. Under the contemptuous gaze of the market porters and lorry men we challenged the mongrel dogs for the scraps. We turned them into vast bowls of soup for the lads.

As time went on, Singer, noticing our efforts to supply food, offered to help. He dried out of his own accord and started to work for us. Eventually I transferred him to the Simon Central Office to help me during the day. For two months he was a tower of strength in the office, organising the jumble that came in, supplying me with hot chocolate and meals, and enjoying every minute of the fifteen-hour work-day I enforced on him.

During that time he told me a little about himself. He was an Irishman and during the war had been in the

Commandos, fighting the Japs in Malaya. He was modest about his army career, but from the hair-raising stories he narrated, he was no coward. I discovered that his downfall had been fighting, and that he had just come out of prison having done five years for manslaughter. He was amusing to listen to, and I enjoyed the short breaks I had with him, listening to his horrific stories. Unfortunately, one night when he left the office he never came home. Apparently he came across an old friend who had taken him for a drink, and within days he was back on the ramp drinking meths. Just before Christmas, when he was very drunk, he fell into the ramp fire. He was found in it twenty-four hours later, his left leg burnt right through. It was amputated. I visited him as regularly as I could manage and I had promised to go and see him on Boxing Day.

"Hi, Singer! And what have you done to the nurses this time?" He grinned gleefully.

" 'Ello, Sal darling." He hauled me down and smothered a kiss on my cheek. "I'm leavin' Thursday, yer know." I appeared surprised though I did know, for Sister had told me some weeks previously.

"Don't blame them, Singer, they've had to put up with you two months now. It's quite a strain you know." He chuckled quietly. "Are they moving you to Roehampton for a wooden leg?"

"Nah, Tooting, to a alcoholic ward. Don't wanta go wivout Betty." Betty was his meths-drinking girl friend.

"Why don't you try and persuade them to take Betty with you?" I suggested. He brightened at this. "Would you like me to have a chat with Sister about this?"

"Would yer, Sal darling? Yer know how it is, we've been together for sixteen years. She and Tommy were my best mates. Yer remember Tommy McGeachy?" Indeed I remembered him. Thomas had been the undisputed leader of the group that used the ramp and Running Water bomb-sites. I remembered the care he took of his men, the trouble he took supervising their living arrangements. Stoking the ramp fire, frying the fish heads for them, patching the holes

94

of the shelter with cardboard. He was arrested stealing two legs of pork for them, and died in Brixton Prison two days later. Alone. Away from them. But they did not forget him. Neither could I. He was a bum and he knew it. He was a saintly sinner, who cared more for others than he did for himself. In looking after them he had a string of convictions for petty offences. He had bummed in the States and Australia and had been on the jake for eighteen years, yet always remained quiet and courteous. He was an incorrigible rogue, but his quiet consideration and kindness left their mark on every soul. For this his subjects made him king. For this we revered him, and sorely missed him. It was on a drizzly June morning that, attended by a Catholic Prison Chaplain, mourned by one Anglican Brother and a Simon, Thomas was laid to rest; no fuss, no commotion. A pauper's grave, for he died alone in prison. There was a wreath from 'his boys'— they had managed to steal enough money for that.

"Yes, Singer, of course I remember . . ."

"He was the most courageous man I've ever met." True praise from Singer.

"I also remember the time you came down to the Simon shelter and as you came in you took off your hat and blood poured down your head."

"Yea, some f . . . bastard had clobbered me one. Oh, we've had a good time. Remember all the cups of chocolate I made to keep yer awake through the night?"

"Dear Singer, I couldn't have done without you then." We continued to reminisce until it was time for me to go.

"Promise me yer'll see Sister about Betty coming to Tooting." I promised, and also agreed to come over to see him. This I did. We managed to get Betty over there too, thanks to the co-operation of the Welfare people in the London Hospital. But all was not well, for I found him in a locked ward. He was sitting by his bed with his peg-leg, grinning sheepishly.

"And now what have you done, Singer? Can't trust you an inch out of my sight, can I?"

"Yeah, I've lost me parole." He had escaped into town one evening and met a freind who gave him some purple hearts, and with a couple of drinks inside him, he was well away. He giggled as he continued, "And then seemingly I threw me crutches away and hopped up the High Street, and kept falling down on me stub. Of course, I can't remember nothing about it. I just woke up next morning when everyone was out, looking for me crutches." He broke into more guffaws.

"Singer, it's not funny; it was thoroughly irresponsible of you and you ought to be ashamed of yourself." He was hooting with laughter.

"Yer should 'ave seen their faces, Sal. They tell me I threatened to kill one of the staff . . ."

"Well, I'm sorry I can't share the joke. In fact I think I've wasted my time coming to see you. Damned if I'm going to make the effort, when you have no intention of trying." I rose stiffly, and Singer was pulling me back.

"Oh, Sal, don't be like that. I'm sorry, but yer know it's hell in 'ere and I ain't had a proper drink for months." His eyes were solemn and pleading like a naughty schoolboy trying to talk his way out of a beating. "Honest, Sal, I won't touch another. Believe me, I won't let yer down."

"While you're locked up like this you won't have much chance," I replied.

A week after this episode I met some of the beats down at the Mission in Orange Street, where every Sunday night we were all given free food and free cups of tea. The same faces were there every week—to con, to grab, to take as much as they could. This Sunday was no exception, and I was there too!

"Hi yer, Kiddo. 'Ow's life been treating yer?" It was God. I could never quite bring myself to call him by this name, it repulsed me and his looks just made me want to vomit.

"Hello there, how's yourself? Fine, though I wish it wasn't so cold."

"*Ciao*, lassie, have a good Christmas?" It was Doc.

96

Morning – a derry by the Thames

Collecting firewood in the 'caves'

Conning vegetables in Covent Garden market

Preparing for the night round – tea from a stall on the Embankment

Waiting for a junkie friend outside the all-night chemist

Morning on the ramp

Night on the ramp

"Yes, you missed a terrific party."

"Hi there, Sal," Jimmy was shouting across the crowded room. I waved to him. I saw Scots Geordie and Brazil Nut forcing their way through a crowd towards me. "Got a fag, Sal?" he asked when they reached me. I produced one for him and gave one to Brazil Nut. She was looking tired and sick, her hair was unbrushed and greasy, and her face was dirty. I wondered what she had been given to make her so drowsy. The music started up, and we found ourselves some chairs. A great cheer arose as the food was produced, and as soon as a plate was put on the table it was emptied before I had even put out my hand. The sandwiches were stuffed into their pockets or under the tablecloth, the plate was removed and then they were shouting again. "Here, over here Missy, we haven't had any here." Another plate was put in front of them, and again the food had vanished and they were attracting another person pretending they had not had any yet.

"Sal, can I have a word with you, it won't take a minute?" Doc was saying.

"Sure, Doc, what's the trouble?" It was hard to hear oneself talk above the taunts and jeers of the beats as an evangelist gave his testimony of how he had been saved by God.

"Well, Sal, we were wondering if you were going on your rounds tonight and if we could come?"

"As a matter of fact I am, and I also have the use of the car, so there would be no walking. Sure, I'd love to have your company. We'll leave here when it closes, about ten-thirty."

Doc gave me the thumbs-up sign and returned to his table where he sat with Twizzle and Carlos. "Third time lucky," I said to myself.

"Wot d' yer say, Sally?" It was Keith, the registered drug addict.

"Hello, Keith, nice to see you. Where's Denise?"

'She's gone to scrounge some more food off the evangelists. Sal, we were wanting to talk to you. You being a

Christian an' all that ... Well, we wondered if you could put us up and a few of the others. Freddie and Scouse and Jimmy were wanting to join us."

"Join us where?" I thought I knew what he was hinting at.

"Well, Sal, it's like this; we feel you can help us, and we want to come over to you."

"Come over where?" I asked cautiously.

"Well, we know you haven't got a place but ... well ... we wondered if you'd get one for us. We'd do anything you tell us. We'd take it from you, because if you preach to us we know you mean it."

I took a deep breath. "Keith, you want me to get a flat for you all, so that you can come off the road?"

"Yeah, that's it. And Jimmy suggested we could look after your dossers, while you went out to work." He had it all tied up. "You see, Sally, I couldn't work to start with 'cause I'm on the junk, and Scouse couldn't 'cause he's on the run like Jimmy, but we'd do anything in the flat you wanted. Honest, we'll pull our weight."

I was silent, not because I had not anything to say, but because he had 'jumped my gun'! I had been turning such an idea over in my mind for some time, but I knew that before I could start such a project, I would have to find myself some kind of permanent employment. It had been with this in mind that a few days previously I had approached Task Force for a job. I had intended to wait a month for my first pay before pursuing the idea or even mentioning it to any of the boys, but now that Task Force had agreed to take me, and Keith was standing before me, I felt that four weeks was too far off. "Let me think about it, Keith. I don't promise anything, but I might be able to do something in that line for you."

Doc and Twizzle were waiting for me.

" 'Ave yer got the car?" Twizzle asked.

"Yes, why?"

"I was thinking; we could earn ourselves a bit of bread."

"How?"

"Well, you have the car with the engine running, while I

98

go up to a spade and ask if he'd like a dirty woman for the night for ten shillings. He's bound to say yes, and when he gives me the money I make for yer car at the double."

"No thanks, Twizzle, I don't want a brick through it. It's not mine."

I took them to all my usual hide-outs and across the bomb-sites, and we spent twenty minutes talking to the lads on the ramp. Doc and Twizzle were nervous at first, for they had heard the rather frightening reputation of Cable Street and how people were beaten up in the East End. As we drove back to Trafalgar Square at two in the morning Doc was saying, "You know, Sal, I've been on the road for eight years all over the world, and I've never seen anything quite like what I've seen tonight. I thought I'd seen everything, but I'll never forget tonight. God, I wish all the beats could have seen this, they would bloody well realise how lucky they are. It would shatter them, don't you think, Twizzle?" Twizzle was himself shattered and was speechless.

"Sal, what do you need to help you in your work?" Doc went on.

"Volunteers to start with. Money, food, blankets, candles—you've seen the needs yourself tonight without me having to tell you."

"I'll get you those things, Sal."

"Well, thanks, but don't do a Robin Hood for me—no stealing, please," I exhorted.

"No, I have friends. When's the next time you're going?"

"When I can next afford it. Probably in the middle of the week."

"I'll be in the Lamb and Flag. Come and get me, will you?"

"Okay." I was thrilled. If only he could take it over from me eventually, and organise a proper group to take over the responsibility for them; to make sure they had enough food and clothing. To take the sick ones to the doctor and to help the really elderly ones to get firewood and other fuel; to patch up the holes in their walls and to find more suitable seats for the ramp. If only I could bring about a closer link between the young beats and the old dossers. If only I could present it in the form of a challenge. At least I could supply them with the opportunity, and enthuse and encourage them to befriend these lonely neglected people. If only I could harness the hidden good-will the beats gave to one another. It would reinstate a sense of purpose into their lives in place of the aimless boredom among both the young and old. There would be a sense of being wanted and needed. If only I could awaken that dormant desire to be of service; if only I could give them an urge to help other people. Preaching was not the answer, only example. If I could have them living with me, observing me, following me, wanting of their own free will to be and do the same things as me, then give them the reins and fall into the background only to be there as an adviser should they want it. Was it in my power? No, but it was in God's power.

Over the next week I prayed about it and thought about it. I knew I was not earning enough money to support them all, but this seemed the least of my worries. I had not in fact come to any definite decision about the flat when one of the beats came up to me to tell me that Chicko was missing and that the latest rumour was that she had taken an overdose. I combed the hospitals for her only to find I was out of luck —though as I did not know what name she would have given and I had just wandered through the wards until I got myself thrown out, I did not do too badly. I searched five hospitals before giving up. I met her next Sunday at Orange Street. She was on heroin. When she saw me, she blushed with shame. "Don't give me it, Sal; I'm on main-line stuff."

"I won't give it you, love; you know you're being a fool. I can't help you unless you're prepared to help yourself."

"No, I get too much of a kick out of it, so f . . . off."

"Okay, love," a leather-jacketed kid grinned at Chicko's language.

"Who's your boy-friend?" I asked.

"That's Tiny. He's just come over from Ireland. Been here ten days."

"Hi! Nice to meet you." I offered him my hand; he looked at Chicko to see whether she approved or not.

"Ah! Go ahead, Sal's all right. She won't preach unless there's real cause."

"So Chicko's showing you the ropes. You're in good hands but don't follow her on to main-line stuff."

Chicko giggled. "You're too late, Sal, he's on it. I gave him a fix yesterday."

"Well, I hope you're proud of yourself, love. See you, take care."

I shoved my way through a crowd of beats and up the stairs to the street. I felt sick. He could not have been more than fifteen, and within ten days of being in London, he was fixing. If only I had a flat now, I could whisk him away. For three hours I trudged the streets aimlessly. I was tormented with my own inability to do anything about it. I knew then and there I would have to make a decision whether to postpone acquiring a flat until I was more financially secure and more fully planned for the event, or to start looking now and muddle my way through. I decided upon the latter, for my sins.

The following night I came across Tiger on the verge of suicide. She was frightened; she knew the police were looking for her, and this prevented her from walking the streets with her chums. A Greek was paying her five pounds a night to stay in his room, and I knew she was earning every penny of it. She was sick and lonely, having lost her self-respect, and did not know where to turn. "I don't want to live another day, Sal, not like this. What can I do though, he pays me well, and I daren't be on the streets at the moment?" The poor kid grasped my jacket, pleading with me. I felt sick and frightened for her.

"Look, Tiger, if I can get you in somewhere will you go?"

"Yeah, if you promise they won't give me away."

"I promise. Now I'll take you over by car. We'll have to walk over to fetch it. It's not very far." She began to hesitate.

"Where yer taking me then?"

"Guildford. I have a friend who'll look after you, and she won't split."

"Nah, I'm not going out of London." She shrugged herself free.

"Look, Tiger, either you want help or you don't! Now which is it?"

"I'm not leaving London," she replied obstinately.

I was annoyed, but quietly I replied, "Okay then, I have a friend who'll take you in. But if you muck him about, I'll never lift a finger to help you again. He's got some of your mates already."

"Is he one of them Christians?" she sneered.

"As a matter of fact he is. But don't worry; he won't preach to you." We had reached the car, and once again she hesitated. I bundled her in before she could run off down the road, and we began to drive towards Crystal Palace. I kept up a fruitless chatter all the way, hoping to relax her, but she sat there with her hands clenched and trembling. With the headlights of oncoming cars, I was having to concentrate fairly hard on my driving, and as I always imagine I'm on a racing track, I was speeding at over fifty miles an hour. I did not hear the click as she opened the door to throw herself out, but I felt the sudden rush of air. Her head and shoulders were out as I made a desperate grab for her. I felt the car heave on to the pavement and I heard the brakes squeal as I jammed them on. In an instant I had to decide whether to keep my hands on the wheel or hold Tiger down, for she was now hanging half in and half out. I must have put my faith in God, for I found myself hauling her back on the seat. I hit the windscreen as we jerked to a halt in fourth gear, and Tiger was thrown on to the floor. Shakily I got out of the car. It was facing in the opposite direction, its nose not two inches away from someone's front room window. Two children clung to each other a few yards away.

"You all right?" I asked with a trembling voice. They were too frightened to speak, and tears poured down their white faces. I saw a figure go into a telephone booth on the other side of the road and it pulled me together. I could not afford to get involved with the police with Tiger in my car. I jumped in, slamming and locking Tiger's door, and with one movement reversed on to the road and was away before any onlooker could have got through to the police. I just prayed that no one had had the sense to take my number. Tiger was whimpering on the seat beside me as I drove towards Crystal Palace. My fear had turned to anger and I became quite voluble: "Tiger, if you try that again when you're in my car, I'll do it for you, you bloody idiot. Go ahead and kill yourself—I'll give you a helping hand—but don't you dare involve other people. You nearly killed three people with you then." She was crying openly now. "If you feel the same now, I'll take you somewhere where there are no spectators and you can do it very quietly and quickly without anyone seeing, and I'll just drive on as if nothing has happened. You won't be missed."

I pulled into the side of the road and waited for her to stop crying; my anger had subsided but it made me no less harsh. "Now, I want a decision from you. Either you want to see tomorrow, and then I'll take you to my friend, or I will accommodate you by taking you on to Wimbledon Common where all the best people commit suicide. And I promise I won't tell a soul." She looked up to see if I was smiling. It was the last thing I was doing. "Come on. Stop snivelling. What do you want me to do? It makes no difference either way to me. Wimbledon Common or Crystal Palace?"

She sniffed, and wiped her nose on her sleeve. "Crystal Palace," I was relieved to hear her say. So with one eye on the road and with the other on Tiger, I took her to my friend. He agreed to take her in on condition I looked for a bed-sitter meanwhile.

Next morning before work I was scanning the advertisements in the papers for accommodation; I must have rung at least a dozen agents, but none of them were suitable. Either they were too expensive for my weekly wage, or they wanted to see her personally which would have been fatal. During my lunch hour I walked round the newsagents looking in their windows, but with no luck. For three days I continued searching, but on the fourth day my friend reported that he had been forced to throw her back on the road because she was a trouble-maker and a bad influence. My first reaction on hearing this was to rage round the office like an angry bear. Friends, they call themselves, I screamed to myself. But as the day passed and it became less important, I began to recognise this as the reaction of any normal person. Millions in his place had thrown out, expelled, got rid of bad influences; one automatically did not want to become involved with 'bad' people, the responsibility was too much, so they were removed. My friend's reaction to Tiger was absolutely normal. Did this make me abnormal. Quite suddenly I was worried. Had I lost perspective? Had my love for these people unwittingly become their downfall? Was I acting like an overdoting mum, spoiling and coddling them? It was my turn to be frightened and lonely. I needed advice quickly, unprejudiced advice.

That night I wrote to Lady Henriques, who during the war had founded the Bernhard Baron St. George's Jewish Settlement with her husband. I had heard her broadcasting the week before, telling the listeners of her memories of London's East End during the bombing raids. I had been fascinated by her reminiscences then, and now I felt that she was the best person to help me. I wrote with little faith, for she was not only a very busy woman but a very important one, and I presumed such letters as mine would be passed on to a secretary and would be accordingly answered. I was shattered when two days later I received a handwritten reply inviting me to tea. Since I was working till six this was eventually changed, and it was decided that dinner would give us more time to talk.

It was a very shy and unsure person who arrived at the Settlement that night to dine with the very wise and grand old lady to whom so many owe so much. I was greeted by Lady Henriques herself, muffled up in an apron and waving a wooden spoon at me, dripping mushroom soup over the parquet flooring. "You're early, child. Never mind, go and give yourself a sherry and sit yourself down."

I was ushered into an office which was cluttered with ancestral antiques and fading photographs and dowdy filing cabinets. Scattered around were green plants, some just sprouting from their pots, others bending rather dubiously in the midde as they jammed against the ceiling. They brought life into the brown room. Beautifully leather-bound books filled the bookcases, intermingled with drab ancient paperbacks. Lady Henriques appeared. She had changed for dinner. "I'm afraid I've had a disaster with the fishes. I've burnt their bottoms." I chuckled with delight. We ate a simple dinner, without the fishes' bottoms, and only when we were at the coffee stage did I reveal the cause of my letter.

"Well, I'm thrilled you wrote to me," she said. "Please excuse the salt spoons in the coffee saucers, but most of my silver's gone. My husband had your habit of mixing with down-and-outs, and he always brought them back here; and every time they came, more of my silver went." She smiled good-humouredly. "Now tell me how you first started in this work." I told her everything, ending up with my concern about the young drug addicts. She listened quietly, occasionally interrupting to ask a question. Her face was grave throughout, her eyes piercing mine. When I had finished we sat in silence for a time. She seemed to have gone into another world, completely unaware that I was no longer talking.

"Well my dear," she suddenly said, "the Lord has used you for this very special work. He has given you the vision and you must not let Him down. Obviously you have the vocation and the resilience that is so necessary, for this work is very demanding as you have discovered. At your age you shouldn't have those mauve lines under your eyes; you must learn to look after yourself as well as others. Taking care of oneself is a much more difficult task you know." I acknowledged her wisdom. "My child," she continued, "you have succeeded with stage one: identifying yourself with them so that they now respect and trust you; at the same time you have gained the knowledge and understanding that you need. This is excellent, but now you must prepare yourself for stage two instead of jumping into stage three as you are proposing to do." I frowned with confusion.

"You don't understand, do you?"

"Not really," I admitted.

"Child, you are intelligent enough to realise that this problem is far too big and far too advanced for you to handle single-handed. Yet you are now trying to open a flat for them and support them. This is not helping them, this is condoning them. The first step you must take is to help them regain their self-respect; you won't be doing this if you leave them to lounge around at home whilst you go out and slave yourself in order to keep them alive. They must pull their weight too. Now if they go out to work and pay their whack of the rent and food, then it is an excellent idea and I'll take off my hat to you and in time, so will they. By all means get them a flat and live with them then."

"Lady Henriques, they won't work. I'm flogging a dead horse."

"Then dear, refuse to find them somewhere to live; what is it you want to do for them—get them off the road? Or get at the root of their trouble, which is fixing?" How sensible she was.

"What role do I play now, then? Just play for time?" I asked.

"No dear, you must move on to stage two—recruitment."

"Recruitment?"

"Stage three is when you have enough money or enough backing to open a house for them. But when that time comes you must have enough young dedicated people like yourself to run the establishment. You see, the burdens and responsibilities and emotional strains are so vast that they cannot be put on to one pair of shoulders. You must, during the next year, find people with your drive and dedication to help you in this work, so that when stage three is possible, nine or ten people, sharing the same vision, will be able to mobilise a pilot scheme together, and then you won't be worn out by the age of twenty-four. During this coming year, continue mixing with them so that they can go on trusting and believing in you, and of course it is important you don't lose contact with them. At the same time interest your young friends, recruit doctors, lawyers and people who could help you in the future. Spread the word that when you have saved enough money you will know that you have the best, and only the best people behind you." How wise she was; how foolish I had been. "Of course, you will find this year frustrating; you will feel that you're not doing anything practical, but remember child, don't rush God. In His own time He will let you have the money you require and not before. Work hard, save as much as you can, keep with them so that you can continue learning, but recruit as fast as you can. God is with you, and well ahead of you too!" She smiled sweetly and put a hand on my shoulder, "And my child, don't try and force your way ahead of Him."

The message transmitted to me was as clear as the six o'clock news headlines. I left Lady Henriques without ever showing my immense gratitude to her. Her words were ringing in my ears as I passed the ramp that night, and the little prayer book she had given me was grasped with pride. In time to come I was to read an extract from it every night, and if I was in a derry with the lads, they would listen respectfully and repeat the words after me. Lady Henriques' prayer book became our evening meal!

Five days later, I was with Keith and the boys at Duke's.

"Found a place yet, Christian?" someone asked.

"No," I replied and continued firmly, "I've decided that I really can't afford to get a flat. My money just wouldn't keep you all."

"Don't worry about that, Christian, we'll help you out there." I knew what he was implying.

"No go, buddy. Before I fork out, I want to see you working." The shattered expressions on their faces made me want to laugh. Keith forced a grin.

"You're joking, work? I've never done a stroke of work in

all my life. And anyway I can't, I'm registered,' he excused himself.

"No, Keith, I wasn't joking. I meant that. We're all equals. I'm no better than you; if I can work, you can work."

"Man, I'm sick. Don't talk daft, Sal."

"Yeah, yer gone mad or somethin'?" Jimmy butted in.

"Nope; I'm as sane as the next man. I agree, Keith, you can't work at present, but you can go into hospital and get yourself well and fit for work, can't you? Anyway that's my final decision—no work, no flat." I walked away, their glazed eyes following me out of the pub. I wondered where I went from here. Should the next move be theirs? It was like a game of chess, but there was more at stake for me.

The following night we were all in Duke's; nothing was said, nothing was mentioned. We all went on to the Alphabet and then to Coco's. At about three in the morning I discreetly left by the back door and wandered down to the Embankment. I loved the winding Thames at night, the street lights reflecting over its massive waters, the rolling shadows of towering, overpowering office blocks. There was a great stillness in the air. I tried to pray.

"'Ello, Sal, wot yer doin' with yerself 'ere, lookin' like Cleopatra's Needle?" Dirty, fat and flea-ridden, with his stringy beard and horse-like hair, Kelly stood before me.

"My old pal, my old beauty," I exclaimed and hugged him.

He squashed me so tight that I thought he was going to break one of my ribs. "'Ow are yer, darlin'?" Kelly was passionate in every way!

"Fine, love; where have you been these last few months?"

"Over new ground; did a bit of 'bird' up in Nottingham, but they released me a month ago and I've been wandering down here since."

"You old fraud; and you never let me know. Come and have a cuppa at Joe's; we haven't been there together for about a year."

"Orrite. Won't be amiss if I do—I pay, of course."

"Of course," I agreed. "In kind or kisses?"

"Darlin' wot d'yer take me for, a millionaire? Kisses of course."

"You wild sexy Irishman—always penniless." I pretended to grumble.

We reached Joe's stall and I bought him a tea; we stood over the brazier toasting our hands. He produced a dog-end and offered it to me. "Keep it, Kelly, I've kicked the habit." He lifted his eyes to heaven.

"An' wot other foolish things 'ave yer been up to whilst I've been away? Ye'll be sayin' in a minute yer don't like the old tipple."

"You know I don't drink you old rogue." I gave him a dig in the ribs.

"Yer know, Sal, I do all the things yer don't want me to do and yer never tell me off. Is it because yer a Christian and that's yer philosophy?"

"It's not a philosophy, Kelly; it's more simple than that. Christianity is the fellowship of love and you can't truly love without forgiving."

"Yer barmy, but yer great with it, kiddo; 'ere take these and give 'em to someone who don't mind smoking with yer Lord." He pressed his packet of cigarettes into the palm of my hand. "Ta very much for the cuppa, Sal. Perhaps I'll meet this 'ere Lord of yers one day and 'e'll do to me wot 'e's done to yer. But 'e won't want the likes of me." He picked up his bundle of rags and sadly slouched away.

I called after him: "Kelly, He wants the likes of you more than anyone else." The words drifted into the night as Kelly had done. I hoped he had heard them. Poor Kelly, poor, poor Kelly.

I made my way back to Soho. I was ambling towards the Alphabet, engrossed in my thoughts, when I saw Tubby running down the road. For Tubby to run I realised that something was seriously amiss. I shouted at him to attract his attention. He waved frantically. I quickened my pace. Tubby was blowing hard, his face was red with exertion.

"What's up?" I asked, as I drew up beside him.

"It's Reg and Ponce, they're fighting."

"That's not unusual," I commented. This did not unduly worry me.

"They've drawn knives," Tubby squeaked.

"Knives?" I responded sharply.

"Yea, and they mean business, Sal. Stop 'em, they won't listen to us."

"Lead on, Macduff." We ran some hundred yards up an alleyway to a basement flat. As we descended the steps, female screams could be heard, and abusive language cut the brief silences. I entered the semi-dark room. Several of the junkies were standing round while Reg and Ponce faced each other, their knives poised, the long evil blades flashing. Someone shouted, "Ponce, lay off him. Come away!" It went unheard. Reg, with a ripped coat, suddenly charged. The knife flashed towards the other's chest. Ponce seemed to leap to the side, and with a jeer brought his own knife down towards Reg's neck. People screamed with terror. Someone knocked the knife from Ponce's hand. The two fighters were sprawled in the centre of the floor with one knife. A friend of Reg's neatly stepped forward and clouted Ponce across the head. Shouts of indignation from Ponce's supporters, who fell upon the victim and it became a free for all. I stood watching completely baffled until someone punched me in the groin. I doubled up with pain and anger but it produced the best result in the end. Furious, I grabbed a chair from nearby and bore down on the room swivelling it from side to side. I scattered groups of fighters. With a blood-curdling yell, I hurled it against the wall where it crashed explosively into smithereens. I looked around for another, and there was the faithful Tubby with another one. I yelled at the top of my voice, "Coppers" and crashed the second one against the opposite wall.

It had a startling effect. Everyone became quiet. I stood trying to look composed and said in a breathless voice, "If you don't belt up, you'll have the coppers down here." I heard a gasp behind me and turned to find Reg creeping towards me. "Yer f . . . well stop interfering, yer bitch." I saw the knife when he was almost on me. I was just too frightened to defend myself, let alone run. I felt the blade hit me as Ponce leaped at him. The knife fell to the ground. Someone was pulling me to one side and telling me to lie down. I felt ice-cold with fear. Some of the junkies were holding Reg down. Tubby was picking up the two weapons. Ponce was kneeling on Reg's arms, sitting across his chest: his hands were wrapped round Reg's neck. "No, no!" I stuttered and crawled across to him. "Leave him, Ponce, he didn't mean it."

Ponce looked at me. His face was a mask of hatred. "Sal, 'e would 'ave killed yer, and 'e ain't gettin' away with that." His fingers tightened their grasp. He was probably right, but it had been a moment of impulse and not a meditated act of violence. I struggled to my feet, and with all my strength grasped Ponce by the neck. He went red in the face as he tried in vain to breathe.

"Ponce, this is what it's like to be strangled alive." I gripped harder. "And this is no impulse so you couldn't get away with manslaughter. It would be a murder charge." I let go and he began to breathe heavily. His hands round Reg relaxed. The terrified faces around relaxed also. Reg, though his eyes were closed, was breathing again.

"Right, the party's over. Let's get out of here before we're shopped," I suggested. Some of the boys lifted Reg to his feet and helped him into the fresh air. Ponce glumly hauled himself upright and without another glance took his leave.

Tubby was fingering my sheepskin jacket. "Yer were lucky," he said, pointing to a tear where the knife had caught me. "Bloody lucky, in fact," he mused.

"The Lord was with me, thank God," was all I could reply.

CHAPTER NINE

It was Good Friday. A day of prayer and fasting, a day for spiritual recollection. I sat alone, lonely, watching coaches draw up on Westminster Bridge and excited foreigners filing out with their cameras to photograph Big Ben and the Houses of Parliament. It was the beginning of their Easter holidays, as it was for the millions of others I had watched driving bumper to bumper in slow procession out of London. The occasional doddery couple, too old and forgotten to join the vacational drift to the country, passed me on their way to church. I followed their example.

The last month had been hell. I had been feeling a little fragile for some time and had had a very bad cough since Christmas. Determined at the time that it was a mild dose of flu that I could walk off, I continued my gallivanting down to the ramp and Soho. The beats began to comment on my facial appearance; I began to look pale and drawn, and my cough became deep and husky. As the spring came on I became optimistic; with the warmer nights I would start to feel more myself. Alas! I was under a misapprehension. I forced myself to continue my East End visits and to help the beats whenever I could, but now it was a burden. I became bad-tempered and only had to climb a flight of stairs to find myself utterly exhausted and breathless. One Sunday night I was with the beats at the Orange Street Mission when the Youth Leader, an evangelical pastor, approached me. He took me aside, thinking I was a drug addict.

"I've been watching you for some time," he told me, "and somehow you seem different from the type of beatniks that come down here. How come you're in this mess?"

"I'm in no mess," I assured him emphatically.

"Are you a Christian?" he demanded.

"Yes, as a matter of fact I am. I was brought up a Roman Catholic."

"You come from a good home, don't you? Do you keep in touch with home? Where do your family live?"

"Around and about," I replied airily.

"Why are you on the road then?"

"What's wrong with being on the road?" I demanded defensively.

"When you're mixing with people like this, there's plenty wrong girl."

Still I offered him no information, but I could not hide a fleeting smile.

"You look sick, are you on the needle?"

"Nope."

"Where are you sleeping?"

"Around." He must have realised then that he was wasting his time pumping me, so he brought the rather one-sided conversation to an end with, "Come and see me next Wednesday at my home, here's the address."

I did turn up when the time came, though I had had second thoughts. His home was in Norwood, where his wife ran a guest house. I spent the evening with them, telling them of some of my real work; intermittently I shoved in the odd lie as a protective barrier. I hoped that in the end he would not know what was truth and what was fantasy. I wanted to remain an unknown quantity until I knew more about him. In the past it had always paid me to be one step ahead of the enemy, and the pastor before me was no exception. During the evening it transpired that he was a devout evangelist and that his life's dedication was to save souls. Brother Vic was a little man with a pale fox-like face and he preached the word of God with fiery passion. His direct manner was frank and forthright. He withheld nothing and yielded everything. His methods to help the drug addicts were contentious, I thought, but he was sincere and he believed that what he was doing was right, I respected him for this.

The next time I saw him was at one of his meetings in Victoria where he talked about the sins of drug addiction and homosexuality. He told me nothing I did not know.

The meeting ended about ten-thirty at night, and only a few remained behind chattering. I wandered out into the street feeling very weak and sick. I had walked a hundred yards towards my car when I had a very bad coughing fit. To regain my breath I sat down on the kerb. I was still sitting there an hour later when two coppers came by. "Hey-ho, and what have we got here—Little Girl Lost? What's your name, Dearie?" I did not answer.

"Where are you going? You can't stay here."

"Nowhere."

"Where have you come from?" the other asked.

"Nowhere."

"What are you doing here then?"

"Nothing."

"How old are you?"

"Over eighteen," I assured him.

"Where are your parents?"

"Somewhere I guess," I said unhelpfully.

They looked at my torn jacket and my soleless shoes. "I think you'd better come along to the station."

"On what charge?" I asked.

"Well, if you don't come of your own free will, loitering with intent."

"Loitering with intent," I laughed. "There's no man in sight except you. I have no intent, nor am I loitering. I was feeling sick so I sat down for a rest."

"When did you last sleep?" One of them lifted my chin and saw the dark shadows under my eyes. "Come on, up you get." I was lifted to my feet.

"Hold your horses." I had an idea. "If you go down to the hall down there, someone will vouch for me." I hoped Brother Vic was still there.

The hall was closed, but one of Brother Vic's evangelistic followers was just getting into his car when he saw me. He came over.

"Do you know this young lady?"

"Yes, sort of."

"What's her name?"

"I don't know," he admitted.

"We're old friends," I butted in, "I see them every Sunday night down at Orange Street Mission."

"What's his name then?" the policeman asked me.

"I dunno." I confessed.

"You're old friends and you meet every Sunday, and neither of you knows the other's name. Who's trying to pull the wool over my eyes?" the policeman said good-naturedly. "Come on, dear, we'll take you to the station and perhaps we can sort out who you are there." As I was led away between the two policemen, the evangelist shouted after me, "Don't worry, I'll ring Vic."

"Tell him I've been loitering with intent," I shouted back jocularly.

At the station I was put in a little room and told to empty my pockets. I did with the exception of my driving licence which I had managed to slip into my bra when supposedly scratching a flea under my arm! The station superintendent was brought in to view me and give me the heavy father act. "Now my dear, a few details. You don't want to have to stay in a cell for the night, do you?"

"Not really," I agreed.

"Well, then, I want your full name and age and where your parents live. Have you run away from home?"

"No. Actually I'm quite innocent." He was gazing at my eyes. "And I'm not taking drugs either," I confirmed for him.

"How long have you been on the road? Some time, by the look of you," he concluded. "Come on, what's your name?" His tone had changed from a friendly note to a brisk business one. Gone were the kind, understanding eyes. "Your name, I said," he repeated. I realised that if I lied I would be in deep water, yet if I did not lie I would be in twice as deep where my own family was concerned. If only Vic would ring, he could stand surety for me. The superintendent turned to the constable. "You'd better call Sergeant Rastle, she's in the canteen."

"Yes, sir." The constable disappeared. Trouble was brewing up.

"Sally Dobbie's the name," I said unhesitatingly. "My parents are abroad, so I live with my uncle in Wanstead. He's Colonel Dobbie, headmaster of a grammar school. You can ring him, he's on the phone." I gave the colonel's number and prayed that he would play the game. Sergeant Rastle appeared and sat with me whilst the superintendent made the phone call. Through the half open door, I heard "I have your niece here." I felt myself blush, and simultaneously I crossed my fingers. "I hear she lives with you since her parents are abroad," the voice continued. I put my hands over my ears so that I did not have to listen to any more. The superintendent came in smiling. I wondered what the colonel had said to him to put him in such a good humour. "Colonel Dobbie doesn't exactly verify your story, but he says have you got your car here? If you haven't he'll come and get you?"

"I have, thanks. Can I go now?"

"Yes," he waved his hand and added, "What sort of car have you? A Bentley?" I was relieved to leave the station on such good terms. Trumps up, for Colonel Dobbie I thought.

Even after this episode, I avoided facing the fact that I was sick. When I had a pain in the chest I put it down to being unfit, but I never sat down on the kerbside until I felt better. Some nights I could not breathe, and the pain was so fierce that I did not know where to put myself. I refused to give in, thinking foolishly that to be sick was a weakness, and whatever the cost I must remain on my feet. The cost nearly became irreparable.

I had arranged to meet Brother Vic and his assistant, Brother Eric, at eleven-thirty one Saturday night to take him to the ramp and round the 'Skipper' sights of London. He had said he wanted to see the dossers and the meths drinkers because he realised that these people were what the beatniks of today would become. So I showed him. Six men and one woman were lying in the ash of the dead ramp fire amongst the bottles and rats. Nine men were lying in the cold smelly debris of the bomb-site caves, and eighty-nine lay prostrate, staggered, or sat hunched in Waterloo

Station. When I dropped Vic and Eric that early morning we prayed for them and that our young beats should never have to follow in their footsteps. I completed the prayer with one of my coughing fits and sat doubled up over the wheel of my car fighting for breath. I then heard Vic and Eric praying for me.

I slept in the van that night, but sleep came fitfully. At one part of the night I felt as if I were fighting for my life and the next minute I lay back numb and as weak as a baby. I wondered whether I would see the morning and then I found myself laughing, crying, convincing myself that I was being ridiculously dramatic and that my sickness was psychological. Again I found myself doubled up with pain, coughing and vomiting, and the fear of death crept in. I wondered whether to crawl out on to the road, but I knew this would mean hospital, being disciplined to a bed possibly for some time. What would happen then to my dossers and my prayer meetings with the beats? I had got so far, I could not stop now. So I lay there, shivering with cold, and perspiring with heat, one minute determined that I would be fine in the morning, and the next terrified of dying. Even prayer seemed little comfort. I tried to visualise the pain our Lord suffered at His crucifixion, and comforted myself that He at one point thought His Father had forsaken Him.

Morning did eventually arrive, and needless to say I was there to see it! The light of day took away the fear of death and I was able to doze fairly peacefully. In the afternoon I went to a meeting, but I was making so much noise coughing that I had to come out in the middle. Once again in the van I doubled up, fighting to breathe. I began to drive round hoping this would take my mind off my sickness. I found myself in Brixton. Half-way to Vic's house, I thought. It was a miracle that I reached his house without crashing the van, for on my arrival my knees were buckling under me and my head was whirling. I staggered groggily in. I saw the figure of Vic's wife. "Could I borrow a bed for a few hours?"

"Of course. Somehow I thought you'd be here today. Vic was very worried about you last night." Thank God she was expecting me, I thought. I was bundled into a bed and told to stay there. Before Vic left for the Orange Street Mission that evening he came into my room.

"How are you feeling?"

"Much better, thanks." I tried to give a vivacious grin, without success.

"You'll stay here till I see you in the morning. All right?"

"Sorry, not a hope. I've got to meet someone tonight." I could not let the lads on the ramp down. I had always brought them food on Sunday night. "And anyway I'm meeting a bloke out of Pentonville in the morning."

"Can't someone do it for you?"

"Nope, he wouldn't let anyone help him except me."

"Okay. You know you're very sick at the moment?"

"Not really; I've got a bit of a cough that's all—nothing serious."

"Come on, girl, who's kidding who? You're very sick." I said nothing. "Will you promise me one thing, that you'll come back here tomorrow?"

I hated committing myself, but underneath I knew it was the most sensible commitment I could possibly have made. At about nine-thirty that evening I crept out and made a very laborious way to the ramp where I spent the night watching over the lads to see that they didn't fall into the fire. I was outside Pentonville Prison first thing in the morning to meet Big Jo.

"Hello, Sal, thought yer wouldn't let me down." Silently I thanked the Lord that he had given me the strength not to stay at Vic's house last night. "Got me fixed up any place?" he continued.

"I'm sorry, Big Jo, I've been so busy I haven't. But if you come with me, I thought we'd go to St. Luke's and see the warden together."

"The alcoholic place?"

"Yes, they're awfully nice there and the warden's a first-class chap." He began to hang back. "Oh please Jo, don't give me any trouble. I just couldn't take it today." I was not sure whether it was the distressed tone of my voice or the dried haggard expression on my face that caused him to say roughly, "Yer okay, kiddo? Yer look as if yer overdoing it. 'Ere 'ang on to me." He gave me his arm.

St. Luke's accepted him, and at last I was in the position of keeping my promise to Vic and had a clear two days ahead of me in which I had nothing specific to do. On the coming Thursday I was a witness in St. Marylebone court, so if Vic would have me I had the rest of that day, Tuesday and Wednesday to get myself on my feet again. I dug into my pocket to see how much money I had for bus fare—I had returned the van to its rightful owner last night. Of course I was penniless, having bought Big Jo some breakfast. I glanced at my watch. It read nine-thirty.

I had a long walk to West Norwood, too long for my sick body. Within half an hour I was vomiting, and my legs were like jelly. Beads of perspiration were falling like tears down my cheeks. My haversack, which I had picked up from Charing Cross left luggage department earlier that morning, weighed heavier and heavier. I was gasping for breath, my chest was one searing pain. Sheer force of habit made me go on. Blurred faces seemed to bear down on me, noises bored through my head. The pavement was moving like an escalator, and the buildings around seemed to be crashing down on top of me. On and on I drove myself until all pain had gone. I was completely numb. My legs weren't holding me any longer. Someone was tearing out of her house towards me. I had a great sense of being closed in. The pavement hit me, the clouds descended and the woman was standing over me. I was walking again, the woman's voice was piercing me to consciousness. I was lying on a bed. A woman was pouring water down me. How I wished it was brandy! She was wiping the perspiration from my face. I opened my eyes and tried to focus them on my surroundings; it was all hazy. Her voice was coming at me again. "Shall I call an ambulance, or have you any family near here that I can ring?"

The word ambulance brought me out of my state of mental obscurity.

"No, Vic, I must get to Vic. Must keep my promise."

"Yes, dear, is he on the telephone so that you can ring him?"

"Yes, I'll telephone him." What a brilliant suggestion, I thought. The telephone was right beside the bed, but for the life of me I couldn't find the finger holes with the letters and numbers.

"What's the number, dear, and I'll dial it for you." What a kind woman she was, full of magnificent suggestions and so sweet with them.

"Hello is that you, Vic? Sally here. I'm afraid I can't make it, I'm sick."

"Where are you?"

"I don't know, hold on." Turning to the woman I asked, "Where am I?"

"153 Trinity Rise, Tulse Hill." I repeated it over the phone to Vic.

"I'm coming right over." The phone went dead.

"He's coming to pick me up," I told her, and fell back unconscious.

The next forty-eight hours I drifted between consciousness and unconsciousness. When Vic got me back to his house he had to get Jean, a nurse who gave up her career to join the evangelists, to help carry me in. Vaguely I remember Jean propping me up as I coughed uncontrollably; other faces were also there, faces that I had seen down at the Orange Street Mission, but then they faded into the wall and I was asleep again. Someone was feeding me. Darkness. Was I dreaming, or could I hear breathing? I groaned. My mouth was so dry from coughing. The nurse was there, she was giving me something sweet and moist; it was delicious. The ceiling was coming towards me again. It was light, someone was wiping the perspiration from my head with a damp towel. There were other people in the room. I began to cough, and my chest burnt as if on fire. Then all was darkness again. Singer and Betty were on the ramp but somehow I could not get there. Every step I took towards them took me a step further away.

"I'll get to them," I shouted. My arms were caught tight and I began to fight myself free. The harder I fought, the firmer the grip became.

"You're not going any place today," a man's voice came through. I opened my eyes. I was in bed and a man was holding my arms, Jean was beside me and behind her was Vic. "Okay, Sally?" he asked.

I nodded.

"Then relax, so Eric doesn't have to hold you down."

The man let me go and began a prayer of thanks. I shut my eyes and fell into a deep peaceful sleep. I awoke next morning to find Jean had brought me a large cooked breakfast. "I want everything eaten up, you haven't had anything solid in you since you arrived," she instructed.

"You bet," I replied. "I'm famished." The door opened and Eric came in.

"That's a good sign," he approved. "So the patient's on the mend?"

"Yes, the fever's left her," Jean answered.

"The Lord is the greatest healer," he said, disappearing.

"How long have I been here?" I asked Jean.

"This is your third day, and we've had quite a time keeping you here. You've kept trying to get back to the ramp. We've had to have someone with you every minute, after catching you sneaking out the first evening you were here."

"Truly? I can't remember a thing."

"No, you wouldn't. You were delirious. Now that you're conscious, you won't do a bolt for it, will you? You won't get very far if you try, because you're very weak."

"No, I won't."

"Make a promise of it, then I know I can trust you."

"I never make promises if I don't think I can keep them and I don't want to risk this one," I replied honestly.

"That's what I was frightened of."

"How long will I have to stay here?"

"Another week and then a week's convalescence." I gasped.

"You've got a hope!"

"We'll see what Vic says," and the conversation halted there.

As the days passed, I grew stronger. I was still coughing, but the pain had eased up and I felt much more ready to cope with life. The rest had obviously done me good. The more revived I felt, the more unsettled I became with my own inactivity. I had a great sense of urgency to return to the ramp. Vic must have realised this because repeatedly he told me that Colonel Dobbie was keeping his eye on the boys there. But still this did not put my mind at ease. In my bones I felt there was something wrong. "Give it to the Lord," the evangelists kept saying. I did, and then took it back! Giving it to the Lord, telling Him all about it did not seem good enough. It did not seem practical just to tell Him and leave it in His hands. The more I prayed, the more perturbed I became. Vic had stayed pretty silent, he was watching this spiritual battle but to date had not felt it was necessary to interfere.

The time came when I packed my haversack and got dressed—I was going to the ramp. Vic entered my room "Going somewhere?"

"Yes, to the ramp. Sorry, Vic, but I've got to."

"Sally, stop doing what your will wants and instead follow God's will."

"I do; you don't think I've spent the past four weeks existing from one day to the next for my own sake?"

"No, you're quite right there; I believe you've been working for God."

"I'm quite sure that I wouldn't be alive to tell the tale now, had it not been the Lord's work," I replied confidently.

"Yes, Sally, but there's a difference between working for God and working with Him—you have yet to learn to work with Him." I was dumbfounded. I had no answer. "Let's pray, shall we?" Vic said.

We got on to our knees and we prayed. My heart was burdened when Vic left me. I took a walk and paid a visit to church before returning to Vic's. This evangelical pastor had hit the nail fair and square on the head. I saw Vic as

I walked in. "Is there a prayer meeting tonight anywhere?" I asked.

"As a matter of fact there's one at Denison House. I'll be going, do you want to come?"

"Yes please," and as I accepted my heart became light like the sun shining. I knew I was half-way to the answer.

The prayer meeting was very evangelical, but no less inspiring. Denomination be blowed, it was the ultimate aim of finding a closer union with God that interested me, and here I found it. The words "When I am weak, then am I strong," pounded through my head. The realisation that until self-reliance is shattered to bits, until we despair of ourselves, we go around trusting and believing in our own powers and in consequence do not employ the power of God. My own failures were not due to my weakness but to my neglect to employ God's strength. I came away knowing the answer to my mental and spiritual sickness; it was not to be found in bemoaning my shortcomings, but in striving to place my trust in His hands. If I clung to God without fail, I would advance without failure.

I stayed with Vic and his family for about a month until I moved into a flat with Jean, and then she decided to go abroad and thus gave the flat up. Once again I was on the road, but in a much better physical and spiritual condition. I passed my nights either on the ramp or down in some grotty club in Soho; now that the summer was here, I joined the beats in St. James's Park where we slept all day in the sun. If it rained, we moved into the tube stations or back to our familiar resting haunt, the National Gallery.

It was on such a wet May day that, in my jeans and leather jerkin, I lounged into the art gallery for a quiet kip. I hailed some familiar bearded faces and moved on to a less conspicuous seat where two youngsters sat. People were milling to and fro, gaping at the pictures or frowning with disapproval at us. I was just about to close my eyes when two ordinary men in sports jackets and neatly cropped hair caught my attention. They were facing one of Turner's sea pictures, but were hard in quiet conversation. There's a saying amongst us beats, that we can smell a copper anywhere; and I didn't have to smell these two—they stuck out a mile. I was about to get up and casually walk away when they came over to my seat and began talking to the two scruffy kids next to me. Now, did I risk getting up and walking out and by so doing drawing attention to myself, or did I sit tight and hope they would pass me by? Quite suddenly I engrossed myself in the picture before me; I leaned forward with a 'cultured' expression on my face and verbally 'ahed!' my appreciation of the great hanging masterpiece. My view was suddenly hampered as a man in a sports jacket stepped in front of me. Under my nose he shoved his dirty little card that gave him all the power he wanted. In a big strong voice he said, "C.I.D."

"So what?" I replied in an equally big, strong voice, and hung my head to one side so that I could continue studying the picture. But I knew I had burnt my boats for getting away. I felt his hand clutch my jerkin, and he roughly pulled me to my feet. "George, we have a funny girl here," he remarked, and addressing me he said, "You'll be laughing on the other side of your face back at the station."

"You threatening me?" I answered viciously.

"No, just making a statement. Come on." He pushed me ahead of him.

"What's the charge?" I demanded.

"No charge at the moment, but we'll accommodate you with one."

"Get lost." I shrugged my shoulder free from his hand. It came back with a grip that was twice as firm. "Okay, mate, I'm not a jail bird yet," I said, freeing my shoulder again. He took the hint, but kept within a hand's grasp of me. I noticed George was bringing the two youngsters along behind me. People watched us curiously as we were paraded from the highly respectable National Gallery in the direction of Charing Cross Station. I waved across at Big Bill and Gipsy Jason who were astride the fountain wall.

"Keep moving!" My jailer shoved me forward as I tried

to stop to say a few words to Brazil Nut and Judy, who were passing.

We reached the railway station. George had now taken the lead with his two frightened catches. We halted in front of a green door. George knocked on it, and I heard the heavy, unmistakable steps of a policeman as he approached the door and unlocked it. "In you go." I was pushed into a bare room with three desks and a few tinny lockers. George, the older and more humane of the two, took up his official position behind the desk, whilst my jailer kept a firm hand on me. He was determined I wasn't going to escape despite the room having no windows and the door having been locked behind us.

"Full names, please, and your addresses," George ordered his now thoroughly dejected captives. They mumbled something, and George produced a little black book. "Well, you're not on my list of London layabouts, so you'd better have a good reason for being in the Gallery," he said, after fingering through the C's and S's. C. mumbled something further and S. agreed wholeheartedly with the excuse. George lit a cigarette and sat back, staring thoughtfully at the two petrified boys. Gently he warned, "If you're on the run, save me the trouble of checking up, will you?"

The boys shuffled uncomfortably. No word passed their quivering lips. My jailer beside me broke into a satisfied smile. Livid at his sadistic streak, I broke out, "That's made your day, hasn't it?"

"Not yet—not until we've booked you," he replied cuttingly.

"That's enough of that, David," George interrupted sharply. "Now lads, who should I ring up to say you're safe?"

"B—— Remand Home," came the sullen reply. Ten minutes later they were put in a black maria and driven away.

"Now, ma'am," he turned to me. "First, you can give me your name."

"Sally Trench." George reached for his black book of London layabouts. "Oh I don't think I'll be in that." I tried not to sound too indignant.

125

He checked. "No, you're not. So you're new to the Square as well?"

"Not really. I drift from district to district actually."

"Have you an address?"

"No. N.F.A."

"Where are your parents?"

"I don't know," I lied.

"What were you doing in the Gallery?"

"I was about to have a kip, actually."

"Didn't you sleep last night?"

"No."

"Where did you spend last night?"

"The Spit and Fizz." His eyebrows shot up.

"Not a very suitable place for any young lady, especially you."

"Why especially me?" I knew my accent had startled him.

"Well, you're obviously from a fairly good family."

"What in your terms makes 'a fairly good family'?" He ignored me.

"You know that place is full of prostitutes and queers?"

"Well, the queers wouldn't look at me, would they? Yes, as a matter of fact I did know—and drug addicts and lesbians," I added.

"What were you doing there, then?" my jailer suddenly shouted.

"I didn't think you'd keep quiet for much longer," I taunted.

"Watch your tongue!" George addressed me sternly.

"I often go there," I replied.

"What for?"

"To get out of the rain."

"Not to pick up drugs, of course!" Sweet sarcasm from my jailer.

"Want to search me?" I challenged.

"You know we can't do that, Miss Trench." George's temper was fraying. "I think you'd better come with us, all the same."

I was ushered out and into a parked Wolseley opposite

the station. We drove in silence to K—— Street police station, my jailer sitting next to me in the back seat. The sergeant on duty put me in a little room on my arrival; it was small, and had no window for escape. There was no fireplace, and the only pieces of furniture were a table and two drab chairs. I tiptoed to the door and peered through the keyhole, sure enough they had placed a constable on duty outside. It was all so dramatic that I had to laugh. I slumped into one of the chairs and went through my pockets; the only form of identification on me was my driving licence which I shoved under the heel flap of my shoe. I was only just in time, for a policewoman entered. Her uniform covered a portly figure, one that I would not like to get on the wrong side of! Her eyes were mistrusting and well shaded by her long lashes; a thick braid of black hair coiled twice round her head was held together by pins and kirby grips. Her voice was pleasant, but had a hard ring of authority about it.

"I'd like you to answer some questions, please." She sat herself in the opposite chair and began writing on her charge sheet.

The routine questions that I had been asked at Charing Cross Station were repeated, and so were the answers; the interview was icily polite on both sides. In the middle we were interrupted by a woman police constable entering; she was gaunt and had a tawny tint to her skin. I was politely introduced.

"Now, Miss Trench, would you kindly undress?"

"What the devil for?" I rudely demanded.

"We want to search your clothes," was the cold reply.

"What if I refuse?"

"I shouldn't if I were you; we don't want to have to use force."

One by one my garments came off until I was standing in my underwear, feeling most embarrassed, especially since I hadn't washed it lately in the Charing Cross toilets! In fact I was so aware that they were not Daz white, but dirty grey, that I apologised for them: "Sorry about that, I

127

wasn't expecting visitors." Their faces remained masks of unemotion.

"Take it off," the younger one ordered.

"What! My underwear too?" This was going a bit too far.

"All of it."

"But I'll get cold standing here naked," I feebly pointed out.

"Go and get Miss Trench a blanket, Constable."

Wrapped in a grey blanket I sat on the chair whilst they searched my clothes; they knew their job and were thorough, very thorough. Every hem, every cuff, every lining was expertly fingered as they sought for some kind of concrete evidence with which they could charge me. My driving licence was found. "This yours?" I was asked.

"Of course, it's got my name on it, hasn't it?"

"That doesn't mean it's your real name."

"For crying out loud, do you believe anything anyone says?"

"Miss Trench, we're only doing our duty," I was stiffly told. "You may get dressed now. When you are ready the constable will take you downstairs. I'll be along to see you later."

"Look, what's the trouble now? You've searched me, and I'm as clean as a whistle. Can't you let me go?"

"I'm sorry. I'm not satisfied yet." She left.

"Satisfied with what?" I repeated the question to the constable.

"I suppose she's not sure whether you're telling the truth," she said.

"So she's gone to check up?"

"Yes, I should think so. Are you ready?"

"Sure, I'm ready for anything now."

I followed her out of the room and down the dimly lit corridor. The occasional uniformed policeman passed us, but paid us no attention. She opened a cell door. Three solid brick walls faced me. On the left was a bunk with a straw mattress, on which lay two grey blankets neatly folded. The cell was tiny, neat and clinically clean.

"Would you like a cup of tea?" the constable was asking.

"On the house, I presume?" I sneered. I had hated tea ever since my boarding-school days. "Okay, I'll have a cup— without sugar." The door slammed behind her. I took off my shoes and paced the uncarpeted floor. I sat on my bunk and studied the spotless walls. I stretched myself out and put a blanket over me. Underneath it I felt protected. All was quiet. There seemed a hopeless finality in the silence of the tiny enclosed room. It was an unnatural silence—not the usual comforting absence of noise. I turned over. I felt frightened. "Don't be an idiot, you've done nothing wrong; they're only frightening you, they've got nothing on you." Listening to my own voice comforted me. "You're innocent. They've only taken you in on sus." I convinced myself. The silence seemed to swallow up my voice. I wanted to scream and tear it apart, but instead I lay quiet and allowed it to persist. There was no sound beyond the rock-like door. There was no movement. It was as if the building had frozen. "Oh, God!" I cried aloud, but it was stifled in the silent solidity. "God, let me out of here," I cried again. I shut my eyes to hide from the reality of my surroundings. I thought about the words, "When I am weak, then am I strong." I tore the blanket aside, and fell to my knees and prayed.

The melancholy rattle of a key turning brought me to my feet. It was the young policewoman with my cup of tea. "I brought some biscuits down, too; I wasn't sure when you last ate."

"Thanks," I replied gratefully. "How long do you think I'll have to stay here?"

"As soon as they've cleared you, you'll be free to go. If you want anything, just bang on the door." She departed once again into the dimly lit corridor and again I was left alone in the tiny locked cell. I sipped the warm tea and enjoyed it. Funny, I thought, I hate tea. I chewed the biscuits. They were sweet and flavoured with lemon cream. They were delicious. I sat on the bunk warming my hands on the cup. Fear had left me. It had smothered the thin voice of reason, but now I was thinking logically. "Thank God!" I said aloud, and suddenly the full meaning of those words flowed through me. I realised once again that until we despair of ourselves and throw our trust into God's hands, we cannot escape these tortures and infirmities. If we neglect to employ God's strength instead of our own, we will forever fail. The words from the Scripture, 'Without me you can do nothing' and, 'I can do all things in him who strengthens me,' shot into my memory. The cell door was opening.

"Miss Trench, I'm sorry to have kept you. You're free to go. Here's your driving licence." She was smiling at me. The door was wide open. The dim light in the corridor was friendly. "I'm sorry, I do hope we haven't inconvenienced you too much," she was saying, but I was not really listening. I climbed the stairs away from the cells. I passed the affable duty sergeant who cheered me goodbye. I pushed open the swing doors, and then I was in the open, breathing in the vegetable smells of Covent Garden. I had been locked away for nearly two hours; it had felt like two years. I walked down the street smiling at every passer-by. I hailed every lorry driver with a hearty "Good afternoon." I patted every lorry with affection as I passed. I was free.

CHAPTER TEN

I SPENT that night on the ramp; it was like any other night, but I enjoyed it more than the others. Probably because I had triumphed in that cell. My self-reliance had been shattered and I had confided in God and He had brought me through. Singer brought me back from my reminiscences with a loud moan. From the iron milk crate on which I was perched, I could see him lying next to Betty in the ash of the dead fire. Kelly groaned himself awake and groggily blinked at me. He scrabbled around in the dirt and found what he was looking for. He took a swig and it dribbled down his chin. "Want a drink?" He passed me the bottle.

"No thanks, Kelly, and I don't think you need any more." I broke it behind my milk crate. Singer moaned again.

" 'E's sick, Sal. 'E's real sick. Can't yet 'elp 'im?" I had never heard Kelly talk with such sincere concern before. I moved over to Singer, stepping over the prostrate bodies of Paddy and Mac. His face was turned to the ground, whilst his frozen body lay with doll-like stiffness. I rolled him on to his back. His mouth was wide open and spittle ran thinly from the sides of his lips. His matted hair was glued with charcoal and nits. The distant draw to death was drumming slowly, the pulse was weak. He lay unconscious, with his meths-ridden girl-friend sharing the same oblivion beside him.

I dispatched the drunken Kelly to fetch some wood to make a fire. He returned after a while with some long planks of wood. Wondering which building site he had swiped them from, I added them to the blaze I had got going with some cellophane and bits of rubbish. Clearly Singer ought to be got into hospital, but I knew of no hospital which would take him in that loused-up condition. I had tried before on other occasions.

"Yer can't do much for 'im, Sal; e's a goner," commented

Kelly. "Listen, luv, you couldn't fix me up with a pair of shoes? Size eight." How could he think of a new pair of shoes while his friend was dying? "I'll see what I can do," I promised, and he flopped down and instantly fell asleep.

A feeling of helplessness came over me. I began to pray. Singer did see the night through, and when dawn broke, and the light brought life, he stirred.

At five I nipped down to the market and scrounged around for some bruised potatoes and cabbage leaves: on my way back to the ramp I begged some bread off a baker and some water from a garage. I fed Singer the soup from a bottle top. This warm nourishment brought new strength, and as he drifted into a peaceful sleep the bells chimed the hour and the Sunday churchgoers crept into their pews to take their communion. I spent the day with Singer, but as the evening came and it began to rain I began to worry—he would not survive another night out.

At about six I left him, and walked across London to fetch a car; on the way back I picked up a friend, Sue. We were back with Singer an hour later, and half carried him and half dragged him across the ramp to the car. We had difficulty getting him all in, and when we did he overlapped on to the driving seat. Sue meanwhile went back for his girlfriend, who, inseparable from her meths bottle, was staggering towards us clutching it. We somehow managed to push her into the back of the mini, and Sue very gamely climbed in after her. I slithered behind the driving wheel, propping up Singer against my shoulder. Within seconds of the doors being shut, the stench of meths and stale urine stung our nostrils. Furiously we opened all the windows, but even this provided little relief. I drove as fast as I dared towards Cable Street. I jumped the lights and accelerated. Singer was becoming heavy, and his dribble was oozing down my left hand as I kept hold of the gear lever. Betty was having hallucinations in the back and Sue was trying to pacify her.

At last I drew up opposite a derelict building. We waited for some cars to pass, and when the road was clear we grabbed the unconscious Singer and heaved and shoved him towards the empty building. I put my shoulder to the door and it swung open "Dump him here and let's get Betty in before some curious passerby decides to nose around." Sue brought her in while I cased the joint. The front room on the second floor was the warmest, with half a pane of glass still in the window. It also had a fireplace. I found some under-felt on the floor above and brought it down for the two to lie on. In another room I tore down some tattered curtains for them to use as blankets. When I had made it as comfortable as possible, I descended the stairs to collect Singer and Betty, who were both lying on the stone floor in utter oblivion. We bedded them down. Singer was ice-cold, and I could hardly feel his pulse.

"What about lighting a fire?" Sue suggested.

"Not yet. I'm going to leave them for an hour; with their clothes drenched in meths they'll go up in a blaze of flame if a spark comes in contact with them."

I had decided to go to Orange Street to see if anyone there could help. We climbed into the car and left the doors open for the night air to clear away the smells our passengers had left behind.

"They ought to be in hospital." Sue was echoing my thoughts. "Sally, I'm no nurse, but that man's dying."

"The hospitals won't take him in that state."

"Then what about the police? He'd be better off in prison."

"Yes, but he'd suffer all the agonies of going dry and being shut away. Sure it would help him temporarily, but in the long run it's a hindrance rather than a help."

"Maybe, but at least it would give him the medical treatment he needs at the moment."

Sue was right, and I knew it, although it went against my principles. I drove to the nearest police station where I recognised the duty sergeant from my earlier days in Cable Street.

"I thought you'd better know that there are two vagrants in a derry down the road."

"You wouldn't know their names by any chance?"
I wondered if he was being sarcastic.

"As a matter of fact, I do." I told him Singer's real name.

". . . and his girl-friend. Meths drinkers. I know. Thanks for telling us, I'll send a constable down to throw them out."

"Throw them out?" I was horrified. "Aren't you going to take them in?"

"Them! Not likely! Heavens above, we have enough problems here without them coming in and lousing up the place and stinking us out."

I turned away, disgusted. His was a typical reaction, and one I would never understand. He was ready to throw them back on to the street and hasten their degradation, rather than make an effort to find a solution to their problems.

Sue and I pushed on to Orange Street. Vic Ramsey was in full swing administering the Word of God, and the beats were in full swing grabbing at the food that was being given out by his helpers. I was greeted with the usual enthusiasm, and asked if I had any spare 'bread' on me. I saw Flo Dobbie ladling out soup in the far corner, and edged my ways towards her. She greeted me with a dazzling smile that always made one feel good. "How are you, Sal? We thought you might be down here tonight."

"Is the Colonel around?"

"He's sitting over there with two German friends who are staying with us. You must meet them, Sal; I've told them all about you. They're fascinated by your work, especially André, who's qualifying as a doctor."

"A doctor?" I could have howled with joy.

I found the Colonel with André and his fiancée, and explained the situation. They wanted to leave there and then but I was delayed by Paul, who asked me if I could find him somewhere to sleep. Having at last got him fixed up in a pad with another beat, Sue and I led the Dobbies and their German friends to Singer's derry.

The police had not called. The black mass that was Singer was in exactly the same position next to Betty as when Sue and I had left him. I bent over him and felt his weak pulse, and put my hand on his chest to feel his heart. It was dangerously slow. André examined him and confirmed that he was very seriously ill. We discussed the problem.

"There's only one way of getting him accepted into a hospital," I concluded, "and that's to dry him out, clean him up and take him there sober and not leave until the authorities have agreed to take him. He'll be sober in the morning, and probably desperately hungry. If you could bring some breakfast and some soap and water we can clean him up. I've got some clothes in the boot of my car that we can put him into and make him look a little more respectable."

I declined the offer of a bed for the night. I drove Sue back to her flat in Baker Street, and eventually bedded down at 2 a.m. next to Singer and Betty, on some old newspapers I had scavenged from Fleet Street on my way back.

I was awakened two hours later by an unusual noise. There were footsteps on the landing below. Police? No, the steps were slow and shuffling. The door swung open and I saw that it was Danny, extremely drunk. To my relief he turned away and continued upstairs.

Singer didn't stir. I was freezing cold, having given him my jacket as an extra covering. I tolerated it for another hour and then got up. Singer and Betty were still sound asleep and looked as if they would remain so for some time. I got in my car for warmth and drove around for some hours, ending up at the Dobbies' for breakfast.

Over large plates of bacon and eggs we discussed the problem of Singer.

"I think our best hope is to get him back into the hospital where he was before, for another alcoholic cure," I said. "At least they know exactly what they're up against with him."

"Will they have him back, do you think? I gather he discharged himself last time half-way through the course."

"I think that's up to us. We'll have to talk them down. But first we've got to talk to Singer himself. There's no point in doing this against his will. He's got to be agreeable to going back into hospital. If he doesn't stay—well, we will have done our best."

Flo was preparing hard boiled eggs, cheese sandwiches and hot tea, and collecting flannel, soap and a towel.

"What are we going to do with Betty?" she asked. This was indeed a big problem that I had purposely forgotten about.

"You might well ask. She'll be furious with us for taking Singer off. But if she wants a fight, there's four of us."

It took us some time to reach our destination because of the rush-hour traffic, but when we arrived, armed with cigarettes and food, Singer was awake. He acknowledged me in a feeble voice, "Hello, Sal!"

"Where's Betty?"

"She's gone to the ramp to get my crutches. Hello, Mrs. Dobbie."

"Hello, Singer, I've brought some German friends to see you."

Singer shook hands with them and broke into fluent German.

When Betty returned with the crutches, which I had left behind on purpose the previous night knowing he could not wander far without them, we sat round a fire drinking hot tea. Singer was still expounding in German and enjoying every minute of it. I felt the time had come to get down to brass tacks:

"Well my old beauty, what are we going to do with you?"

His answer came somewhat as a surprise. "Oh, Sal, get me away!"

"But where to? No hostel will have you." I hoped he would make the suggestion I had been plugging towards, but Betty interrupted.

"Can you no' get us a flat, Sal?"

"Where are we going to get the money to pay for it?"

"We'll get a job, won't we, Singer?"

"Do you honestly think either of you could hold down a job?" I answered them frankly. "The first thing you must do, buddy, is to get yourself well. You need decent food and good sleep and proper looking after for a week or so."

There was a silence. Each one of us knew what I was insinuating. Singer sadly replied, "I'll go back into hospital if you want and finish that cure."

"Ye don't want to go back into hospital, Singer, you're all right." Betty had begun. For a while they argued between themselves, both tempers rising until I interrupted.

"Look, Betty, you love Singer?" She nodded her agreement. "Well, you know he's a very sick man— don't you want him better?" She looked sulky.

"Look, Betty, luv, I'll come back as soon as I'm out," Singer explained.

"You're not goin' in any bloody hospital." She was really roused now. Turning to me with her fist raised she shouted, "You're not takin' him. You lay a finger on 'im and I'll do yer."

"Betty, don't talk daft," Singer said. "She's only trying to help us."

"By sending yer to 'ospital?" She spat at my feet so that I should realise how disgusted she was with me.

"Singer, the decision's yours." I threw the ball back into his court.

"Well, Sal, I'd go but they won't take me like this."

"That's no problem; a bit of soap and water, which we have, a few clean clothes from the back of the car—they'll have you." I said it with the confidence I lacked. So we set about washing the man down whilst Betty watched scowling from her corner. We washed his nit-infested head, his neck and face. We discarded his shirt and vest and put them on the fire and then washed his almost black chest. We went to the nearest chemist and bought a razor. Whilst André was shaving him, I washed his stinking foot and put a clean sock on it. I scrummaged through the second-hand clothing in the boot of the car and came back with a white nylon shirt, a clean brown V-neck sweater and a sports jacket. As we carried him from the derry, no onlooker would have recognised him as the filthy dosser we had brought in the night before. Betty followed us out screaming curses and insults. As I drove away, I called out to her, "Be on the ramp in the morning tomorrow, and I'll come and pick you up and take you across to see Singer—that is if you're dry."

At the hospital I left Singer in the car with the Germans whilst Mrs. Dobbie joined me to add strength to my attack. The duty doctor was a middle-aged man with a rugged face that was pale and drawn, yet despite his obvious weariness his eyes were alert and sympathetic.

"Well, Doctor," I told him, "I won't beat about the bush. I have an ex-patient of yours outside." I gave Singer's name. "He was admitted about three months ago for an alcoholic cure but he discharged himself a few weeks later; since then he has recognised his folly and would like to return to complete the cure." The doctor said nothing but turned to his filing cabinet and drew out a large foolscap sheet. He studied it for a few minutes before replying. "Where's he been these past few months? On a bomb-site?"

"Yes, we took him off it last night. He's dried out," I added.

"Where's his girl-friend?" How I would have loved to read that record sheet!

'She's in the East End at the moment; at least that's where we left her."

"Last time he was here, she was bringing in meths to him, and finally we had to stop his visitors; how prepared is he to toe the line this time?"

"Why don't you ask him? He's outside sitting in the car." Singer put on a very good show of sincerity. That he was a desperately sick man in both mind and body, I would not have disputed, nor that he really wanted to go through with this treatment at present. But whether after a week of good food and plenty of sleep and no crude spirits he would be feeling so much better in himself—then the test would come, and in my heart, much as I believed that Singer really meant what he said, I knew that it was hoping for too much. "Right, we'll have him in; he's really going to make an effort this time," the doctor was saying to Mrs.

Dobbie. I wondered how many times relations had said it to pessimistic doctors.

From the car I extracted some pyjamas and gave them to Singer. "Yer will bring Betty to see me, Sal?" he was demanding.

It was against my wishes, but I had to stick by my promise. "Sure, I'll bring her across tomorrow."

With that, Singer was wheeled away in a chair and we sighed with relief. "I must dash," I apologised, "I was meant to be in court for one of my lads at eleven this morning; I'll see you, thanks awfully for your help and support."

As I had promised Betty, I turned up at the ramp in the morning. During the night I had found a fifteen-year-old girl on the run from a mental hospital, who had become involved with my beat friends and had taken some drugs and now the boys were ready to take advantage of her. I managed to extract her before they raped her. It then took me six hours of patient waiting before she recovered enough to talk to me. She had run away five days ago and hitched to London where she spent the night in one of the insalubrious dives of Soho until some boy befriended her and took her back to his room. Here he ordered her to undress and she refused. A scuffle followed and she managed to escape; disillusioned, she walked the streets and came upon the wandering beats who shared their bread with her. She followed them to their derries at night and watched them indulge themselves in drug-taking sessions. On the fourth night, depressed and tired with nothing better to do, she joined them and took her first 'smoke'. I found her being undressed by the lads that evening. By the time she had finished telling me her story, she was weeping. I did not sympathise or reprimand her, but let her stew in her misery whilst we drove to the ramp.

Betty was sitting alone on an upturned petrol-can smoking a cigarette. From the empty bottles beside her, I gathered she was far from sober. As I walked across the dump heap, she turned her back on me. I paid no attention but went and sat next to her. "Morning, Betty!" She made no reply. I sat for five minutes staring at the rubble, and then quietly began to hum the tune, "My bonnie lies over the ocean"; half-way through the third time of singing it Betty swung round to face me and addressed me: "Where's my Singer?"

"In hospital. I'll take you to him in the car." Silence. I changed from humming to whistling.

"I ain't cleaned up and I ain't sober," she replied gruffly.

"Both of which can be rectified," I answered. After another minute she swayed to her feet and tottered towards my stationary car.

"Hop into the back, Betty, next to the girl," I said thoughtfully. I noticed the girl's look of horror as the stinking filthy woman clambered in beside her. I smiled to myself, as I put the car into first gear and drove away. "Betty, I'm going to drop you at the Dobbies' where you can have a bath and wash your hair and sober up, whilst I drive this kid back from whence she came."

"I don't want to go no place, I just want to see Singer."

"Which you shall do, but not until you've cleaned up." I changed into fourth gear, and through my rear-mirror watched her fiddle with the side windows; "Let me out of 'ere, I'm not goin' no place." I accelerated. "Let me out!" Betty screamed at me.

"I can't, Betty, there are no back doors to this car." I drove faster.

"Stop the car!" she ordered. "Stop it, I say!" Resolutely I drove on. Suddenly I felt her hands round my neck. With my elbow, I hit her arm away. "Don't be a fool, Betty, do you want to kill all of us and then there'll be no one to help Singer." She sat back in her seat and went into a sulk.

Needless to say, Mrs. Dobbie was wonderful. She welcomed Betty as a long-lost daughter, and found her bath salts and all sorts of luxuries to help pacify her. I drove on to Chelmsford with the girl.

"Where's the hospital?"

"I'm not going back there," she replied defiantly.

"Oh! Where do your parents live then?"

"Don't want to see them." I drove on. In Chelmsford, I drew up outside the police station. "Get out," I said, opening the passenger seat door for her, "we're going over there."

"The police station!"

"Well, you don't leave me any alternative, do you?" I replied. She sat there sullenly chewing over the situation. Innocently, she looked up. "Okay, I'll play fair," she offered. "You can take me home, but you'd better ring them first. There's a telephone box over there." She pointed to one on the corner.

"I wasn't born yesterday." She dropped her eyes and actually blushed. I had been caught before with this one; whilst I'm phoning for them, they run.

"Take your choice now. This is your last chance." Once again she burst into tears.

I let her cry herself out, and then gently said: "Look, kid, you've had a hell of an unpleasant week. Whatever you've got to face now, won't be as bad as what you've just been through, believe me, so take a bit of courage and let's go home." I smiled at her and added, "Anyway there's two of us facing it this time." For the first time she smiled, and I suddenly realised what a very attractive girl she was.

We went to her home and I returned her to two desperately anxious parents. They gave me lunch and told me all about their difficulties with their daughter: how for no reason at all she had refused to eat and become desperately ill, and eventually how after two years the child welfare authorities had stepped in and put her under child care because they said the parents were unable to look after her properly. When she still refused to eat and became ill and difficult, the authorities had put her in a mental hospital. Her father concluded, "You'll never know the anguish it caused us when we were told that we did not adequately give our child the parental care she needed. You have no idea what we've tried to do for her; my wife has spent three hours at a time feeding her because she just refused to eat. After all, the child-care people have done no better than us."

I left a very disturbed family, yet knowing I was helpless

to do any more than I had done. I commenced my drive back to London to pick up Betty. She was sitting there—spotless! Her fair hair sparkled with cleanliness; she had washed, cut and groomed it. Her usually rough face was smooth and powdered, and a slight touch of lipstick matched the delicate rosiness of her cheeks. She had dispensed with her filthy clothes, and now sat immaculately dressed in an outfit of Mrs. Dobbie's. She grinned self-consciously as I entered.

'Woo-ah! Singer won't recognise you," I remarked with delight. "Are you ready to go then?"

"Och, woman, I've been ready to go for hours." I gave Mrs. Dobbie a wink and opened the door for my elegant passenger. Betty talked non-stop all the way to the hospital, telling me all about her youth forty years ago, and how in her day she had been quite a 'peach'. Her mind was quite clear without the drink to befuddle it, and it boosted my ego no end to see her so animated and happy. On our arrival I tactfully let her go up to the ward by herself and said I would follow in about half-an-hour. She tripped up the stairs like an excited teenager going to her first date!

Whilst Betty was occupied with Singer, I made my way to another ward to see Keith who was in for a drug cure. I rang the bell outside the two massive doors of the ward. I heard steps approach, followed by the grating of the key in the lock. It reminded me of the mental hospital I had been in.

I walked past the communal bathroom into the ward. It was all in dull yellow, even the bed heads, except those that were chipped; the mustard coloured lino added to the general yellowness. It was more like a mortuary than a hospital.

"Hiya, Sal!" Keith had recognised me. He was sitting amidst the yellow in yellow striped pyjamas, his long fair hair draped over his shoulders. I began to wonder if I was going colour blind when I saw that his eyes were yellow to match the rest of his surroundings.

"What's the matter, Sal?"

"Nothing, I'm going mad that's all; everything seems yellow, even you."

Keith burst out laughing. "I've just had jaundice."

He had put on some weight and was not looking so gaunt, yet his eyes seemed very glazed for a person off drugs. "How's it going? Get a lot of pain or aren't you going 'cold turkey'?" Once again he burst into laughter.

"Come off it, Sal, you know the signs after all this time." I saw his hand quiver slightly as he put a cigarette in his mouth.

"You're not getting the stuff in here?" I asked amazed.

" 'Course I am; pay them enough and they'll bring anything in."

"Pay who?"

"The male nurses, or the guys that are allowed out, though you have to be careful there, because recently they've been searching them as they come in. Man, you can get anything you want in here, from purple hearts, black bombers, to meths and heroin."

"Where do you hide the stuff when you've got it?"

"In the locker—they never go through our lockers. Here, come and have a peek, I've got the whole 'jacks' here." I peered into the top drawer of his locker and saw his 'works'. I was dumbfounded. "But don't the doctors notice you're high?"

"Well, I'm careful when I take a dosage; I mean I wouldn't be so daft as to take one just before he comes to see me," he explained unashamedly.

"Where do you get the money from?"

"Anyone. Everyone nicks from everyone in here; the other night when I was asleep, some geezer nicked my N.A.B. money from my locker, so the next night I went and nicked it back and took his whilst I was about it."

"But, Keith, what's the point of coming in here for a cure if you're going to make no effort to give the stuff up?"

"Be reasonable, Christian. It ain't fair on a man to just cut him off his only salvation; they've got no idea of moderation. When they eventually cut me right off the stuff, I thought I wouldn't live. Man, the agony of it; as it was I nearly went berserk and tried to kill a bloke, and three of them had to hold me down. You wouldn't understand, you've never taken the stuff," he said, shrugging his shoulders.

"I'm trying to understand, Keith, believe me, I'm trying to understand."

"Sorry, Sal, it's just I've got to have it. Since I've been in here, I have been cutting it down." For me this was no compensation. Still, I could not see how the doctors did not recognise the symptoms; they must have known he was fixing on the quiet.

I felt utterly discouraged as I climbed the steps to Singer's ward; it was all so futile and pointless. Unless Keith was prepared to help himself first, no doctor, no psychologist, no parson could minister successfully to him.

Once again I rang a bell and the ward doors were unlocked. Singer was at the far end, with Betty sitting beside him. He was fairly doped, but already looked more like himself.

"Oh, Sal, it's great to be in a bed; I was at my last tether."

"I know, buddy, you don't have to tell me that; what do you think of your sparkling girl-friend?" Betty blushed.

"She's a chick," Singer replied admiringly. "A real chick." They sat holding each other's hands like a couple of newly-weds; it was incredible how far away we were from that infernal ramp, and to think in half-an-hour I would be returning Betty there—my heart ached at the thought. Yet I knew if I suggested putting her in a hostel she would automatically rear up in opposition; unless she was prepared to help herself, I was wasting my time and fighting a losing battle. If only I could put the idea into her mind!

I looked at my watch. "Well, Singer, I'm afraid I must take your girl-friend from you."

"Where are you taking her?" Singer had given me the opportunity.

"There's only one place where she belongs," I replied harshly. It had the effect I hoped it would. Betty flushed with anger, and Singer rushed to her defence: "Hey, Sal, watch what you say; she's as good as any woman. She's the finest woman here." I looked unconvinced. "Look how smart she can look and, see, she can leave the drink."

"Sure she can, for six hours at a time," I replied provokingly.

Betty was fuming. "Sal, can't you try and fix her up somewhere?" asked Singer.

"Sure if she agrees, but she won't agree, we both know Betty." Betty was nearly falling off her seat with irritation.

" 'Course I will," she replied hotly.

"There you are, she will," Singer repeated.

"You mean that, Betty? Truly? Where I can get you fixed up for the night you'll willingly go?"

For an instant she hesitated, and then said: "On condition it ain't going to be too far away from Singer."

What a sauce, I thought, but I was not going to query it, having reached this far with her. "Fine, right, that's fixed then," I concluded.

"Can you bring her tomorrow, Sal?" Singer asked.

"Yes, I should think so. Come on, Betty, it's getting late. See you, Singer, behave yourself now." I rose and walked away so they could have a few minutes by themselves. Meanwhile, I was racking my brains for ideas; though Betty had accepted the challenge in front of Singer, I realised that within a very short time she would want to back out. I had to act fast and firmly. I knew of no place near Singer that would take her in; all my friends who had flats lived right the other side of London. I knew she would not go into the Salvation Army or Church Army hostels.

Betty was at my side and talking to me.

"Don't 'e look better?"

"Much better. I only hope he'll stick the cure out, then he'll be really on his feet." As I said this, a vague idea passed through my mind. It was a brilliant idea if I could work it right. We got into the car as if to drive away, when I turned to Betty: "Singer was thrilled to see you looking so smart!" She giggled with pleasure. "Won't it be marvellous, if he can leave that hospital a cured man?"

"Och, Sal, it would be terrific," Betty mused thoughtfully.

"He'd be able to get a job, and have some money for some digs, and you'd both be able to go out to parties together."

"And it would all be thanks to you," she complimented.

"No, Betty, there's only one person who can help Singer back on to his feet, and that's the person he really loves and respects." Our eyes met.

"Do you mean me?" She looked surprised.

"Mmm, I do, only you. You could be setting the example after all," I explained.

"How do you mean, Sally?" She was interested.

"Well, to begin with you could also have a cure." I dropped the bombshell as calmly as I could. Her face was a mask of control as she sat there silently chewing it over.

"Where would I have to go?" She was nibbling at the bait.

I played my trump card, "Why not here, so you can be near Singer?" Her face relaxed into a triumphant grin.

"Okay, I'll have a try. When can I come in?" she enquired eagerly.

"There's no better time than now; come on, let's go and see the duty doctor." Silently I sent up a thank-you prayer to the good Lord, and together Betty and I made for the main hall. The porter put us in the waiting-room, and we settled down to reading some crumby magazines. Half-an-hour passed before the porter popped his head round the door to say there was some trouble and the doctor would be a bit of time; another half-an-hour passed, and Betty was becoming fidgety and nervous.

"Och, Sal, let's go. I need a drink!"

"Wait a few more minutes, I'll go and see what's keeping him." Once again I approached the porter who said he was very sorry but the doctor was still being delayed. I returned to Betty, who was now striding up and down impatiently. "He's just coming," I lied, closing the door firmly behind me. In another fifteen minutes Betty had returned to her usual self, swearing and cursing, demanding that we left that instant, threatening to kill me unless I let her out. I tried pacifying her, but it was getting beyond my control as she began to crave for her bottle of meths. Suddenly she

146

threw up her arms to punch me in the face because I was standing between her and the door; I managed to see it coming and ducked in time but still held my position; she swung round and swiftly made for the window. I did a splendid tackle, and brought her down. She was a heavy woman and a dirty fighter, but I was taller, much fitter and perhaps even a dirtier fighter! I managed to sit astride her stomach with my elbows resting on her arms, she lay there squawking with fury but totally unable to budge me from my tight hold. Suddenly the door opened and a wiry, fresh-faced young doctor entered: "Eh—which is the patient?" he asked as I helped the livid Betty to her feet and brushed her down.

"Perhaps you'd like to come into my office. I'm sorry for having kept you so long." Betty, sulking, followed him, and I came up behind her, just in case she was thinking of making another bolt. I explained the position once we were seated, and assured him Betty really wanted to take this cure; I only prayed he was not going to ask why I had been sitting on her.

"Well, obviously, we don't like turning willing patients away," he was saying, "doubly so if it may help another patient."

"Most certainly it will put Singer's mind at rest," I assured him.

"Yes, very well then, I'll make arrangements for her to go to A1 ward." He went out to call a nurse, and I turned to Betty. "Well, Singer's less than three hundred yards away I can't do any better than that for you; the rest is up to you." A nurse came in smiling cheerfully and led Betty away. Without a word to me, she went. Poor Betty!

It was dark outside, and I looked at my watch; it was nine p.m. and time I started on my round on Waterloo Station.

The days seemed to fly, I had so much to cram in, yet not once did I miss my daily visit to the hospital. It gave me great joy to see both Singer and Betty so contented and well as they went from strength to strength. Meanwhile my visits to Keith had to cease when a male nurse told me that drugs were being smuggled in to him and that he was forbidden visitors except his immediate family. With a bottle of orange juice in my hand I tiptoed round to the side, to the window opposite his bed. Gently, I lifted it a few inches and peered in. I could see him in the far bed reading a book; a male nurse passed in front of me and I ducked, hoping he would not notice the window ajar. I hissed Keith's name and the chap in the bed nearest the window turned and stared at me, "What do you want?" he asked.

"The bloke in the far bed over there, please."

"Keith," he shouted, "there's a friend to see you—she's at the window." I could have throttled him for letting the world know, but no irate nurse came running. Feeling like a criminal, I knelt on the window-ledge. Keith got out of bed and came across. "Hi, Sal!" he greeted me. "Won't they let you in either? They found out I was still getting the stuff."

"That doesn't surprise me. Anyway, here's the orange you asked for." I passed it under the window.

"Thanks, Sal, you're a poppet."

"How are things going? You look much better. All the yellow's gone."

"I'm fine now; I'm going to discharge myself tomorrow. I'm fed up with this blasted place; you haven't got a 'pad' have you?"

"You're joking, boy! Even if I had, I wouldn't have you back there, you're much better off in hospital. Why the hell don't you have a real bash at this cure and stop mucking about? You're not being fair on yourself or your doctors, and more important, you're taking up a bed which could be being used for someone who's really prepared to buckle under. I know it's not easy, Keith, but nothing in life is given to us on a plate. We've all got to work at it, that's what life is all about. Why not just give it a try?" I pleaded.

He shrugged his shoulders amiably and replied, "Not me, Sal, I'm hooked good and proper; there's no cure for me, I know that. I'd better get back to bed. Thanks for bringing the orange." Bare-footed he made towards his bed, and as he did so he turned round and quietly said, "God bless you,

Sally." I pulled the window down so that he might not see the tears in my eyes. I had never thought I would hear those words from Keith.

Next day he did discharge himself, and the rumour went round that he had gone home to Bristol, which gave me hope; but before the week was out I saw him coming out of one of the Trafalgar Square toilets, his eyes as glazed as ever.

Every afternoon I spent an hour with Betty and Singer; and Betty would never allow me to come empty-handed. "Sally, I need a brown handbag." "Sally, Singer needs another shirt now that he gets up every day." I lost many a friend taking their clothes from them, in order to provide for my two demanding friends. But it was worth it, just to watch them taking an interest in their clothes. My hour's visit was a jocular one; Singer never tired of telling me his Irish jokes—they were never-ending! I was glad that he could keep us amused and off the subject of the ramp. My hours with Betty and Singer during this period were some of the happiest I have ever spent, yet I did not deceive myself. I waited and prepared myself for the ending.

The first signs of discontent came from Betty three weeks later; she began talking about the ramp and the lads. Singer and I jollied her along, but our efforts were fruitless. The next day Singer was in a filthy temper and I was forced to make the conversation and tell my only two jokes! The day after, I arrived at the hospital to see a nurse approaching me: "Miss Trench, the matron would like to see you." Before I entered her office, I knew the gist of the story. Betty had got out and gone down to town and bought a bottle. She had returned with it to Singer's ward and between them they had consumed it and now, with Betty urging Singer on, they surged down the ward in full flight, cracking one man over the head with the bottle as he tried to stop them, and out they went never to be seen again.

I did not bother to query the small details: how were they able to consume a bottle without anyone noticing, and how did they get hold of the keys to unlock the ward doors?

I did not really care—the point was, they had gone. Though I had been preparing myself for this, it choked me. Perhaps, it injured my pride more than anything and left me deflated. I wanted to blame God and say, "Why did you allow this to happen after all I had done?" And then I realised this was far more of a disappointment to Him than me, for it had not been through my strength that I managed to help Betty and Singer, but through His strength. I was just His instrument and had no right to have any pride. This knowledge helped me, but did not repress the pain of failure.

CHAPTER ELEVEN

SINGER and Betty were back on the ramp again, and there I left them; from previous experience I had learnt that only when meths drinkers had reached the end of their tether and were close to death, did they turn to someone for help; I gave my friends a month of the ramp and then they would be begging for my assistance again. In fact, I was wrong, because a few weeks later they were picked up for stealing milk and brawling and were each given a month. I was glad of the rest!

With five of my meths drinkers now 'inside' I did not visit the ramp so often, but spent more of my nights in Soho; I visited most of the dives and memorised the faces belonging to them. It was interesting to see the same faces night after night at the same dive but as I frequented them more often, I realised that each club specialised in a particular type. One of the most popular drew the homosexuals. It was situated in a dark alley opposite numerous other obscene clubs. It was in the basement and cost five shillings; as I entered, I noted the little fat man, smoking a cigar nearly as big as his head, who gave me my ticket and locked the doors behind me. In fact the doors remained permanently locked unless the little fat man opened them.

I crept down the stairs, feeling rather conspicuous all by myself and entered a dark room, barely lit by the illuminated red bar at the end. Soft seats were round the room and people were dancing in the middle; the continuous loud pop music drummed through one's ears at first, though by six in the morning one hardly noticed it! I parked myself in the corner nearest the exit and just studied the youngsters dancing. Despite my mixing with young long-haired beatniks day-in, day-out, for the life of me, I could not differentiate between girl and boy. They all had long hair, effeminate faces and wore rings. They all wore bell-bottom trousers and long polo-neck sweaters which gave them no shape. The couples all danced very closely, some tickling their partners' necks or scraping their long, painted nails through their lanky hair. Some were embracing and kissing whilst others were fondling each other and swapping love-bites. Suddenly the horror of it all dawned upon me—that they were all young men except for the odd one who had a woman. Watching them making love to each other made me want to vomit. I was still fixed with horror when a young man came and sat next to me. He was completely out of character with his short-cropped hair and tapered grey flannel trousers and sports jacket. He obviously thought the same of me as he looked me up and down.

"Would you like a cigarette?" he offered in a soft Irish voice.

"No thanks, I don't smoke."

"Where do you come from; you're new down here?"

"This is my first visit. Tell me, am I right, are all these people men?" I asked incredulously.

"Most of them—they're all homos." He laughed, "You look shocked."

"Do I? It's funny, I've seen a lot of iniquity, filth and sickness, but it's never made me feel quite so repulsed as this."

"Are you new to London then?"

"No, not at all; I mean I've seen and known many homos but just sitting here watching them make love to each other —ugh!" I couldn't go on.

"Well, what are you doing here anyway?" he asked curiously.

"It's somewhere to sit the night out," I replied.

"Haven't you got a pad? Are you on the run or something?"

"No—just N.F.A."

"You don't add up—a girl of your education roaming like this."

He was referring to my accent. "Well, if it comes to that nor do you? How come you're down here? Don't tell me you're a homo too?" I said.

"No, I've come down to get some smoke; I come every night for it."

"The peddlers are down here then?"

"Sure, most of the guys here are on horse, or pills."

"Don't the police raid it ever?"

"Occasionally, but no one ever keeps the stuff on them."

"Where do they hide it then?"

"In the Gents—here, I'll go and get you some," and he disappeared into the toilet, only to reappear a few minutes later with some hash. "This was hidden on top of the cistern," he explained, "but they hide it anywhere, sometimes in the centre hole of the toilet roll."

"Do you work?" I asked him.

"You joking? Of course not."

"How do you get the money to pay for it then, and keep well dressed?"

"If you come with me, I'll show you."

I followed him up the steps and out into the alleyway. It was a warm, mild night, and it was a relief to be able to breathe in the pure night air. We walked into Wardour Street and moved past the striptease clubs. We came to an open doorway and stopped. "Stand behind the door out of sight and watch through the crack," he ordered. He leaned himself up against the door post and watched the passers-by. He must have stood there about fifteen minutes before he nodded at a middle-aged man walking along the opposite side of the street; he was dressed in an immaculate dark suit and wore well-polished shoes; underneath his suit he was clad in a dazzling white shirt and dark red bow tie. Not a hair was out of place as he crossed the road towards John with a spring of confidence in his stride. At first I thought John knew him, but as I listened to the conversation I realised how wrong I was.

"Good evening, sir," John politely addressed the stranger. "Were you wanting to see a show?"

The man hesitated.

"Your choice, sir, ordinary dull striptease for five guineas or two homosexuals performing, ten guineas, sir; or the best, sir, two lesbians—that of course is fifteen."

"Make it twelve pounds," the stranger bartered.

"For you, sir, I'll make it twelve." John handed him a ticket as he gathered up the notes. "Top floor, sir, door nine."

The man brushed past him and hurried up the stairs. He must have reached the first landing when John grabbed me by the hand and whispered, "Run." We sprinted down Wardour Street and turned into a side road where John halted, breathless with laughter.

"Couldn't be easier, could it?" he laughed.

"Do you mean there are no such shows on there?"

"Of course not, at least not in that flat. Sometimes I just give them an address and put them in a taxi and they go off to it all excited, only to find I've sent them to a warehouse or something." He burst into more laughter. "It's just too easy for words, because when they get there and find nothing, they can't do anything about it or go to the police, and I'm usually miles away by the time they come back to look for me."

"How much do you make a week doing this?"

"Average is about fifty pounds, sometimes less, sometimes more; depends if I can catch the right kind of guy. Usually the best type is the well-to-do frustrated married businessman who's told his wife he's got a board meeting and then comes into the West End for a bit of excitement. There are hundreds of suckers around."

"One day you'll be the sucker when you do it to a copper."

"Maybe. Meanwhile, I've plenty of money and live well—like to come to my pad for the night? We can have a smoke back there."

"No thanks, I'm not that sort."

"What are you going to do then?"

"Probably go and spend the rest of the night in the Spit and Fizz," I answered.

"I tell you, you're safer in my pad than there."

"That's a risk I'd prefer to take. Anyway it's been nice to meet you—in fact quite a revelation."

The Spit and Fizz was reputed to be inundated with young people on the run; I think the main reason was that it was the only club one could go and sit in without having to pay an entry fee or buy a drink. It was grotty like the people who run it, but it had a roof and was a place to sit out of the rain throughout the night. The only rule they had was that no one could sleep there, and periodically a big brawny fellow would come round the benches and kick those who had drifted into sleep awake. Prostitutes wandered in and picked up young kids who did not know what it was all about. Every other night it was raided by the police and they never went away empty-handed. Homos wandered in to try their hand with some new kid. It was the same every night as I watched the child's eyes brighten as the homo stuffed a five pound note in his pocket and then together they moved off. I stayed here till the dawn broke and then took a walk down to deserted Piccadilly Circus. I had just reached Shaftesbury Avenue when a flashy American car drew up beside me; a man in a dinner jacket was at the wheel and his girl-friend, sparkling in diamonds and mink, was in the passenger seat.

"What's matter luv, looking for a girl-friend?"

You dirty-minded beast, I thought, but calmly replied, "No, just a sugar-daddy, I gave her the boot the other day for kissing me on my big toe." They roared with laughter which surprised me.

"That's great—can we give you a lift somewhere, honey?"

"No thanks, I'd prefer to walk."

"Isn't it dangerous for a lone girl, walking the streets at night?"

"Its safer walking the streets than getting into cars with strange men," I replied curtly, thinking this would close the conversation. Instead he laughed again and turning to his girl-friend he remarked,

"Isn't she cute—give her a dollar for her breakfast to-morrow."

I stood there stunned for a minute, wondering if I had heard right. The girl-friend drew a pound note from her purse and gave it to the man. "Here," he said, "I like a girl with spirit. Take this."

I hesitated. "Go on, take it, kid, there are plenty more where I come from," he drawled. I took it.

It was Sunday. Late Night Special was over and the beats were drifting away into the night. I was with Kinky Cowboy and Little Jack who were discussing where they were going to spend the night; Skinny Jinx joined us. We decided to sleep in the York Terrace derry. This large house, behind Madame Tussaud's waxworks, was at the rear of some of the most expensive property in London, fronting Regent's Park. Although it was Crown property, the interior was a complete wreck and had been used as a pad by destitute beatniks for over a year. There was only one snag and that was getting in, for the doors and windows were bolted; if you did not mind heights it was a piece of cake, but if you suffered from vertigo, as I did, it was purgatory. I had done it before, shinning up the long drain-pipe of the house next door, clambering across the flat roof and down into the pad. On this night, though I accompanied the lads there, I was not prepared to do the climb, so I left them as Kinky Cowboy began his ascent.

It was over twenty-four hours later that I saw them again, at three in the morning in Covent Garden.

Cowboy's voice boomed out aggressively, "Why didn't you come into the pad with us last night? Did you know?"

"Know what?" I had not an inkling what he was talking about.

"You bitch, you did know, didn't you?" his eyes were full of suspicion.

"Jack, what's he talking about?" Little Jack was white and drawn, and was twisting his fingers with nervousness.

"The body!" Jack spat out.

"The body?" I repeated. "What body?"

"I found a body." Cowboy's voice had a note of pride in it.

"A dead one," Skinny Jinx added.

"Anyone we know?" was all I could think of saying.

"Yes, but I'm not going to tell you, because you already know." He really believed that I had not followed him into the pad because I knew that there was a dead body to be found there.

It was Skinny Jinx who explained what had happened. "Cowboy climbed over the roof, as you know and he was going to try and let us in so that we didn't have to shin up the drain-pipe. When he was creeping down the stairs to the cellar he fell over something but being so dark he couldn't see anything, so didn't think twice about it. At least not until the morning when we noticed he was covered in blood; so we went down to investigate. The body had been hidden under cardboard boxes and whisky bottles and we could just see this leg hanging out. We would have left there and then and said nothing, but Cowboy's fingerprints were all over the joint where he had fallen. It was a right mess; his head was battered in and the maniac who did it had bound and gagged him; there was blood everywhere."

"Who was the guy?"

"We all knew him as Dave—he used to visit the Duke a lot." I knew many Daves at the Duke. "What did he look like?"

"His face was so battered we couldn't see."

Cowboy, less furious now interrupted, "The police kept us for hours. I bet they think we did it."

"Oh! I don't expect they think you did it Cowboy, after all you did report it. They probably kept you to help with their enquiries."

"It weren't too bad really; they treated us quite well," Skinny Jinx mused.

"Let's get hold of a paper and see if our names are in it; hey, we could make our fortune out of this. Let's go and offer an exclusive story to one of the papers for a price," said the unperturbed Cowboy.

"F . . . off" replied Jack "I don't want any more to do with it."

"Well I'm going down Fleet Street, this'll make us

famous," Cowboy shouted as he moved away. "After all I know who the murderer is." Jack and Skinny Jinx followed him.

It was in all the national papers next morning, though no names were mentioned. By midday the police had identified the body, and his name appeared under the small passport photograph in the *Evening Standard*. I recognised it instantly as a drug addict whom I knew fairly well. I read the brief paragraph over again:

> "Scotland Yard are appealing to beatniks and drug addicts for information about the associates of David G——. He was found dead on Monday morning in the basement of a derelict building."

I sat motionless remembering an incident in Lyons about a week ago. I had been alone drinking a coffee when a tall youth with a college scarf approached me; all I knew about him was his name was Sid. "Sal," he had said to me. "You wouldn't know where that bastard G—— is? He's done me, he was meant to be getting me some pills and he's got my money."

"No," I had replied "he'll probably be at the Duke to-night, though," and Sid left. Later that evening, the rumour was that he had been going round asking everyone if they knew where he could get a revolver from.

That night I wandered the streets, my conscience tearing me apart. I knew it was my civil duty to go and give this information to the police, but I also had a moral obligation to the youngsters who trusted me and gave me their confidence. If I should 'rat' on him and the other beats should find out, my relationship with them would be a closed book. No one had liked the dead man. As one of the lads had remarked in the Duke, he deserved what he got; Sid had not been the first he had double-crossed. By morning, I had decided to give the information anonymously over the telephone. But I was to make a very foolish mistake. Not sure where the murder enquiries were being held, I asked a policeman; instantly, he was on me. "So you've got information, have you? You'd better come with me." He dragged me off to his police box where he rang St. John's Wood police station. My heart sank, of all the places in London, it had to be my own local police station, where most of the policemen knew me. The policeman was thrusting the receiver into my hand, "Here, you'd better speak to the detective sergeant yourself."

"I have some information that might help you with your enquiries, but I have a few complications with it," I explained incoherently, wondering how I was going to explain myself.

"We'll send a car round for you right away," the voice came back.

"Oh, no, please not, that would be disastrous." I could imagine the lads' faces if they saw me being driven away in a police car.

"Well, can you come direct to the station here."

"Not exactly." It was just too risky if my parents were about. "Would it be possible to meet you somewhere else completely? I'm sorry for all this secrecy but I can explain it when I see you." So it was agreed that we should meet outside a tube station in an hour's time. The green Wolseley was there as I came out of the station, a pleasant-looking middle-aged man, whom I presumed was the detective sergeant, was behind the wheel, and beside him sat a young well-built man. As I approached them, the young one got out and opened the back door for me. I climbed in.

The older man addressed me: "I understand you have some information for us regarding the body found in York Terrace last Monday."

"That's right."

He suddenly produced a photograph before I could continue, and said: "Who's this—do you recognise him?" It was a very youthful picture of Dave. I identified him at once.

"Did you know him well?"

"Not exactly, he wasn't a personal friend, but I knew him to talk to."

"When did you last see him?"

"About ten days ago, at the Duke of York."

"When did you last go to York Terrace?" I was slightly taken aback.

"I walked along the road last Sunday with Kinky Cowboy, but I haven't slept there going on three months now. Look, can I explain my position before we go any further?"

"Certainly, go ahead."

I told them everything, emphasising that I would be very grateful if they could keep my visit to them quiet. They were very co-operative and kind, and having written out my statement covering over two pages, they let me go. They asked me to keep my ears open, and stay in touch with them, and then suggested that if I could visit the Soho dives that Sid frequented and let them know if I met up with him, it could be of great help. I made no promises, the last thing I wanted to become was a policeman's stooge.

I was relieved to leave them and return to Trafalgar Square, yet glad I had done the right thing, later that afternoon I bought an *Evening News* and under the caption *Interpol Join Hunt for Beatnik Killer*, I read:

"This afternoon five men and a girl were being interviewed at St. John's Wood police station, after the girl had dialled 999 in the West End and said she had vital information about the murder.'

I wondered if that girl was me?

One afternoon in the Square I met Rex mooching around with a little girl, she was dressed as if to look in her late teens, but her refreshingly youthful face gave her away. "Hi Christian, come and have a coffee?" Rex offered.

"You're feeling in a very generous mood," I commented, for it was the first time Rex had ever offered to buy me anything. We went into a café nearby and Rex told me how he was about to have his first record made. He was very full of himself, and I was forced to let him rattle on for a good fifteen minutes before I could get my say in. "Where's the girl from?"

He turned and looked at the silent youngster on his left. "Dunno—where are you from?" he demanded.

The child blushed and said nothing. "Nowhere," said Rex, "apparently."

"Where did you come across her?"

"Don't rightly know, one minute she wasn't there, the next minute she was, since when she's never left my side."

"You don't want her as a millstone round your neck, do you?" I asked.

"Not really," he agreed.

"I'll take her from you if you want," I suggested casually.

"You're welcome, if you don't, I'll only sell her for a dollar to a Pakistani."

I was glad he was agreeable. When he had finished his coffee, he departed leaving me with the youngster. She had long well-groomed hair and a fair, spotless complexion; her clothes were clean and of good quality.

"What's your name? I'm Sally."

"I thought he called you Christian," she answered in a soft, well-spoken voice. I wondered if I had mistaken her age.

"Christian's a nickname; I prefer to be called Sally."

"I'm Amanda."

"When did you arrive in the Square?"

"What Square?"

"Trafalgar Square. You're obviously a new girl around here."

She did not answer, but blushed again; I tried another line.

'How long have you been in with Rex?"

"About an hour."

"Where did he pick you up?" I knew Rex well.

"In Dean Street, in Soho."

"Lost your way or something?" She nodded the lie.

"Well I guess you're better off with me than a Pakistani." She looked at me in horror. "Wasn't he joking when he said that?"

I pretended to look surprised, "No, of course not, don't be

so naïve." I had plenty of experience when it came to lying.

"What would happen if he had?" she questioned fearfully.

"Oh, he'd do what they all do—tear off your clothes and get at your body." Tears began to stream down her cheeks in disillusionment.

"But he seemed so nice and kind," she pleaded.

"So what! He's still penniless without a girl like you to support him, isn't he?"

"You mean—" When the word came out it was almost swallowed up in shame and distress, "prostitution?"

"Well, of course, what else do you expect? Of course they all end up having abortions, but that wouldn't worry you!" She swallowed and went as white as a sheet as she listened to me rambling on. "Well, what else are little girls made for, especially ones so young and pretty as you; you're what's called a sitting target." By the time I had finished with her, she was a very frightened child indeed.

"Where do you live?" I asked her gently.

"Portland Terrace, opposite Hyde Park."

"Would you like another coffee? When did you last eat?"

"This morning; can I have another coffee please?"

We both had second cups before I said: "Right, let's go."

She shied away from me her eyes popping out of her head with fear. "To my car." I took her by the arm and pushed her ahead of me. Once in the car, I locked the door.

"Are you a policewoman?"

I laughed. "No, you'd be in a mess if I was."

"Where are you taking me?"

"Wait and see; tell me, how old are you?"

"Fourteen."

"Still at school?"

"Yes."

I took a guess. "Convent school?" She blushed again.

"How did you know?"

"I didn't; it was just a guess. What did you come up here for?"

She had lost her fear and was talking quite freely. "I

don't really know; kicks I suppose. I've often seen the people in Trafalgar Square, and think I would like to be like them, free and independent."

"You call it freedom and independence?" I queried. "Where's the independence when you have to rely on other people for your food and money? Where's the freedom when you're being moved on all the time by the police? Where's the freedom in having to con and beg? Where's the freedom when you're caught in a network of destruction and become a slave to drugs or alcohol?" Her eyes were filled with fear again as she wept. She cried: "I didn't realise it was like that, I had no idea . . ."

I interrupted her sternly. "No, and you didn't reckon that I'd find you before you got yourself into serious trouble either. You'd better thank the Lord your luck was in."

We had reached Portland Terrace.

"You're not going to tell my parents?"

"Not this time—but if I ever catch you down there by yourself again, I'll not only inform your parents but also your headmistress at school, and this is no idle threat," I warned her.

She climbed out of the car. "Thanks for bringing me back."

"You're welcome, just don't let me have to do it again," and with that I drove off. But she left me thinking, for this was how so many like her came to be on the road in London. Many from perfectly secure and happy homes saw my young wandering beats demonstrating their so-called emancipation, with no ties or responsibilities, and fell under the deception that this was freedom; and by the time the initial glamour of it had worn off and it had become a drudge it was too late to go home, for the parents had by then severed the relationship. I had caught Amanda in time.

Now that I had been on the road for a year with the beats, I could divide them into three classes; the permanent beat, who never wanders further than the Square or the Duke of York; the homing beat who wanders off for the season or a weekend but always returns to the Square; and the wandering beat who can never stay in the same place for more than twenty-four hours.

The permanent beat was the most obnoxious; he went around owning the whole of London, expecting everyone else to comply with his wishes and know his face. Being in one area they usually slept in pads, having found and worked on a sugar-daddy from the first day of their arrival. All strangers were brusquely brushed aside and taken advantage of without exception.

The homing beats were loyal and patriotic members of the Square, and sucked up to the permanent beats who shared their pads with them if they felt it would be worthwhile. Otherwise they skippered in derries, always returning to the Square in daylight. They usually went about in groups, having met up with other kids from their own town.

The wandering beats were the lone wolves. They were the most tough and most grotty, sleeping anywhere and everywhere; far more self-reliant and having more initiative, they kept on the move; an acquaintance of all and sundry, a friend to none. But whatever classification they fell under, not one had any respect for the opposite sex, and only the very occasional one had any manners. They all blasphemed in every sentence without fail and their minds were pathetically imprisoned with sex or drugs.

When a new face came on the scene, one ignored it until it approached you. That was how Jess first introduced himself to me. He was a tall, skinny fellow, and reminded me of a runner-bean. He had honest eyes and a large generous smile. I was sitting on the steps of Trafalgar Square as the rain poured down. It was evening, and most of the kids had moved off to the Duke of York. Jess slouched over to me and without invitation parked himself beside me.

"Where do you come from?" I began the conversation.

"Channel Isles."

"Arrive today?"

"No, some days ago I got in; been skippering since; what about yourself?"

"Been here a year; come from nowhere and going nowhere," I replied.

"Sounds enterprising!" he commented, and I laughed dryly.

"Come and have some chips, I've just about enough for six-pennyworth."

And that was my introduction to this intelligent and sensitive boy. He attached himself to me without any encouragement on my part; from our first meeting I felt he was an unusual beat, and he became the first and only beat I knew who had any kind of manners. I was also to notice, as time went on, that these began to slip. Within three months of mixing with the kids in the Square, he was swearing like a trooper and had his arm round anything in a skirt. It had not taken long to change him into a completely different boy. I was to discover that Jess had gone to a public school, and was the son of a literary scholar. Unfortunately I never discovered what made him hit the road, but from my knowledge of him it could have been social rebellion.

Another, similar to Jess, was Tony the alcoholic, a tiny unassuming Irishman who, though full of Irish blarney and charm, never managed to con himself some digs. He was young and clean and stood by his principles; he had a derry in New Compton Street, and it was like an obstacle course getting to it! But once there, it was a good hide-out with an old Victorian bed to sink into. Tony was an acute alcoholic; if he was unable to get any conventional form of drink he would not think twice about consuming surgical spirits or eau-de-cologne. Yet when he was sober, one could not be introduced to a more pleasant boy. The times I've picked him up off his face and supported him to some cover and stayed with him for fear of the police picking him up! Sticking like a leech, I've followed him, waiting for the moment when he reached beyond his own strength, and would be forced to call out for my help. Then came the process of drying him out, a process that made him sick for some days, getting him on his feet and finally back to work. I usually had a couple of months' rest before we repeated the same procedure. Tony's drinking problems went back six years when his junkie girl-friend committed suicide and her body was hauled out of the Thames. To hide himself from the horror of realisation that he could have foreseen this tragedy, or perhaps even stopped it, he turned to drink and was soon drinking to vile excess.

Tony's story is like a hundred others and his ruination is like a hundred others. None of them were sick in body, but all of them were sick in mind with a harmful addiction; together I watched them rot, helpless. All I could do was pray that God would keep His guiding hand on them.

CHAPTER TWELVE

"Everybody has a right to be loved." The words were mine, the voice was mine. "We were made by love for love." The kids puffed at their dog-ends, but they were listening; the stench of sweet wine wafted through the darkness as the bottle changed hands.

"Why don't my Mum want me then?" a young voice challenged.

With all my heart I wanted to give Dustie a satisfactory answer but as so many other times before, I had none. "Well then, Sal?" he persisted, leaning over his girl-friend's legs and grabbing at my jerkin, pulling me within inches of his shaking body. In the semi-darkness I could see his puppy-like face was contorted with rage and bewilderment. "Love!" he bleated, "F . . . love. Tell us, Sal, what is love?"

Someone cuffed him. "Lay off, Dustie, leave 'er alone." He released his grip and sat back discontentedly. I watched him draw a syringe from his pocket before he added, "Ain't got an answer 'ave yer, Sal?" He wiped the needle on his shirt cuff. I groped for words.

"Dustie, the meaning of the word love to me is to give. When you stop giving you stop loving. When you stop loving you stop growing." He began to take off his belt and wrapped it tightly round his arm which was scarred with burnt-out veins.

"Love is your passport to life, Dustie." I threw it out in desperation as he plunged the needle in.

"Save it, Sal." Someone was trying to spare me. "We know what yer tryin' to get at and we love yer for it—'ere puss, pass us a fag—but yer wastin' yer time on us, Sal."

"We're done for—there ain't no hope for us," another voice said.

"Ay! Speak for yerself," another piped up from the far corner.

"Who's sittin' on the bloody vino then?" a sleepy voice floated through.

"Can yer no' sleep for . . ." Scottie was interrupted as the door downstairs was smashed open and the heavy steps echoed in the room beneath us. "Fuzz," someone hissed, and without a sound we emerged from our corners and crept towards the back window. In an orderly fashion, we filed out on to the window-ledge and one by one shinned down the drain-pipe of the derelict building which had been our haven for the past week. Without a word or a glance we separated and drifted off into the night, probably never to meet again. Some would go underground, some I would possibly meet tomorrow night, and others would spend it in a cell. They came and they went, young and vulnerable; they passed on hurt and bitter. The night swallowed them up. I pushed my hands into my jeans pockets and deliberately quickened my pace for warmth. I heard footsteps following me and a lanky, sparsely clothed youth drew up beside me.

"Where yer off to, luv?"

"Just walking, cooling my heels you might say."

"Come an' 'ave a coffee wiv me?"

"No thanks mate, don't drink coffee," I cheerfully replied.

"Tea then?" he persisted.

"No mate, don't like tea—nor milk," I added quickly.

"Wot do yer drink then?"

"I don't. What goes in, has got to come out!"

He guffawed. "Yer jokin'."

"No, I'm quite serious, put it this way, it's just more convenient if I don't drink; still, I'll take a hot dog off you," I offered. We wandered through Soho, past the shuttered cinemas and empty theatres.

"On the road?" he enquired.

"Yes and you?"

"Came down from Manchester yesterday, with an empty pocket. Suppose yer dunno any mates who're flushed, like?"

"You're joking!" I replied in return.

"Forget it. I'll see yer around then," and he left me.

Cad, I thought, trying to con another down and out! And

I never even got the hot dog! I turned down Greek Street, where the odd man lounged optimistically out of the shadows as I passed. I peered at my watch under the lamplight. It was three-thirty. It would soon be dawn, and with it came the security of daylight.

"Hey, Sal." It was Sheila. She was panting heavily, and her long tangled hair fell in rats' tails over her face. "Quick help Jinnie." I could see she was very frightened. "She's gone and done herself."

"How do you mean?"

"I was going to my room and I saw her lying there . . ."

"Take me to her," I ordered sharply. We turned back down Greek Street and ran up to Shaftesbury Avenue. "Come on, stop lagging," I urged my friend as she struggled to keep up with me. "Anyone else seen her?"

"No," was all she could gulp as she tried to draw breath. We tore towards the coloured lights of the striptease clubs.

"How long ago did she do it?"

"Dunno, I only just found her a minute ago." She pointed to a doorway and we began to ascend the stone stairs. Sheila had taken the lead, and on reaching the second landing flung the door open. I pushed by her and nearly fell over Jinnie's body. I crouched beside the nearly naked figure and felt for her pulse. She was lying on her back, clad only in her underclothes, on the bare floorboards. Only then did I realise I was squatting in a mass of blood. She looked dead, but I had caught a very weak pulse beat, her body was still warm . . . "Call an ambulance," I shouted to the stricken Sheila, standing like a statue in the doorway. "There's a call box on the corner, dial 999—for God's sake, woman, pull yourself together! Hurry!" The door swung shut, and I heard her descending. I took off my jerkin and covered Jinnie and then I saw the long thin blood-stained knitting needle. I stared at it in horror. I thought I was going to faint. I fought down the nausea and, steadying my hand, I carefully withdrew it. The blood poured out. I crossed her legs, hoping to somehow control the haemorrhage, but it just seemed to pour out all the more. I tore her vest from her back and made it into an absorbent pad. Then I just prayed.

I heard the flurry of steps as Sheila started up the stairs, so I shouted to her, "Stay downstairs and wait for the ambulance so that you can show them up." Thankfully I heard her go down again. Jinnie lay motionless, her thin cadaverous face expressionless. She hardly looked her seventeen years. "Where's that ruddy ambulance?" I cursed under my breath. I found myself fingering the knitting needle and needlessly wiping the blood from it. Of course the police would have to be informed, and so would her parents. They would certainly not want her home now. Perhaps she might not live? It would be the best thing for everyone if she didn't ... Oh, God, what was I saying? But what would become of her.

"They're here, Sal." Sheila's voice forced me back to reality. I strode to the door and blocked Sheila's view. I was not sure how much she had seen previously. From behind her appeared the ambulance men with their stretcher. They lifted the limp body on to it. "You'd better come with us, Miss," one of them said, as his eyes fell upon the knitting needle I was still holding. "The law will have to be informed you know."

"I quite understand. You won't need my friend, though?"

"Who found the body?" He talked about Jinnie as if she were already dead.

"I'll come, Sal, she is my friend you know. I don't mind." So together we climbed into the ambulance. The siren squealed and the brakes were released.

"Nasty bit of work that," the ambulance man commented. "Don't understand what makes a kid do a silly thing like that—what drives them to it?" I could have told him, but I didn't.

"Do you know her?" he was addressing me again.

"Yes, quite well; she's been in London a year."

"Was she ... er ... well ... you know?" It was funny how he was frightened to use the word.

"A prostitute, you mean?" I said helpfully, "Yes, she was."

"They all come to a bad end." I nearly throttled him.

"Is she going to live?" Sheila asked, as he took her pulse for the third time. The sirens stopped as the vehicle halted; the back doors swung open and Jinnie was lifted out.

For two hours Sheila and I waited in Casualty; occasionally we picked up a magazine, but though our eyes read the words, our minds were far away. We paced the corridor, looked up expectantly each time a nurse passed us, and then threw ourselves wearily back into our seats. At last the sister appeared and briskly asked us for details about Jinnie. We gave what information we could.

"Did you know she was pregnant?" she asked.

I heard Sheila gasp with surprise.

"No," I replied. "Jinnie never talked much, and certainly never about her personal life."

"Did she have a steady boy-friend?"

"I couldn't honestly tell you; she had a lot of friends," I hedged. "How is she—is she going to live?"

"She's lost a lot of blood—we're giving her a transfusion now." She rose as if to go but I grabbed her arm.

"That doesn't exactly answer my question," I pointed out boldly.

"Dear, I can't, only the doctor can answer that question," she gently replied and took her leave.

The hours passed slowly. When it was daylight, a policeman arrived. We went through the same rigmarole of questions. Sheila was exhausted and fell into a fitful sleep. I took a short walk in the cold nippy morning before joining her. Just before midday a nurse shook me out of my drowsiness. I wondered what the outpatients sitting opposite me thought. "Miss Trench, Doctor Sage thought you might like to know that your friend is going to be all right." Sheila, who had been aroused by her voice, burst into tears of relief. If she hadn't I probably would have done.

"When she wakes up, will you tell her we were here and we'll come and see her tonight," I asked.

"Yes dear, now why don't you both go home and get some sleep?"

"Yes we will," I lied, and firmly taking Sheila by the arm

171

went out into the sunlight. If only that nurse knew the impossibility behind her utterly reasonable suggestion.

That was the first of seven abortions I had to deal with over the next six months. Some, like Jinnie, survived them; some did not; and those who had, wished they had not. What happened to them afterwards? The hardened ones returned to their old life in Soho and would chalk up a few more; the very sensitive ones suffered the loss of their self-respect, and having only rejected society before, now rejected themselves. If they did not successfully commit suicide, they were placed in mental homes; some were sent to centres administered by the Home Office; the rare case went home.

Sometimes the kids asked me to visit their homes to plead for them with their parents; I always found this disheartening, for I felt that if one had to persuade the parent to have her child back, the child was possibly better off without the parent. Often I found the parent was obviously in a more neurotic state than the kid, and sheer fear of any more problems forced them not to take on this further responsibility. The more I went to their homes, the more apparent the reason became why the kids could not, or would not get on with their families. More often than not, the obstacle in the relationship was not total lack of love, but total lack of trust. It was not helped by neither side acknowledging the others' limitations, or always undermining the other's accomplishments. Every human being is looking for self-perfection and subsequently self-fulfilment, therefore, instead of maturing a relationship by assisting one another, petty jealousies and pride took predominance and the relationship suffered. The more I visited these families, the more aware I became of the frightening responsibility of parenthood. As time went on, I found myself sympathising more and more with the parents, and less and less with the kids, Not being a parent myself I could not fully understand, but I felt the burning desire of a distraught mother to help her sixteen-year-old daughter who had started taking her first doses of heroin and cocaine. Again,

I felt the tears of hopelessness of a father weeping for his son as he was led away to start a Borstal sentence. The cruelty of youth, I discovered upon reflection, was that we expected adults to resolve every problem, overcome every difficulty and make every decision correctly because of their status as parents, and it never occurred to us that they were no more equipped for life than we were. For me it was a shattering discovery.

We were all outside the Duke; it had closed early after trouble had broken out between two junkies, and the police had to be called. I was sitting on my bed-roll, with my back against the wall, dozing. I had not been to sleep for two nights, having spent them on the ramp with Steela Horse, who had burnt off three of his toes earlier that week. I had no idea where I was going to spend tonight. Tiny Geordie, his arm round a girl, came and sat beside me.

"I've got a message from Freddy."

"Freddy? Which Freddy?"

"Freddy the queer. He's going up to Newcastle tomorrow, and should you hitch up there, you'll be able to find him in the Forth Café where they all hang out."

"Thanks. I can't somehow see myself going up there for some time." I yawned, and stretched my legs out across the pavement.

"Where are you kipping?" Geordie asked.

"Haven't really organised myself yet; thought I might go to that derry in Camden Town; I looked in on the one in South Kensington the other night and it was full of Germans and froggies."

"That's miles away; if you'd like to come with Annie and me, you're welcome; it's a lovely derry and not very far from here."

"I'm ready when you are."

"Okay. Annie, shall we go there now?" She grunted something inaudible and snuggled into Geordie's chest. "Wait five minutes, she's a bit tired. She came in from St. Albans today." We continued sitting there.

173

Jess came along and fell over my feet. "Stick 'em in," he shouted as he went on his way; to which some youth replied, "Don't be so vulgar!" and silence once more reigned.

"Come on, Sal, we're off." Geordie was hauling me to my feet and lifting my bed-roll on to my back. On the way Annie managed to con half-a-dollar off an American and we bought a packet of cigarettes from a slot machine.

It was only eleven o'clock when we reached the derelict. It was in splendid condition. Every window had glass in, the door was all in one piece, and some of the rooms even had curtains. "There's only one snag, and that's getting in," Geordie explained. "I'll do the climbing if you stand in the doorway." With the agility of a cat he climbed over the spiky railings and for a second balanced there as he judged his jump over the gap with a twenty feet fall; he landed perfectly on the window-sill and clambered through the top window. The next minute, he had opened the front door for us. "Top floor," he ordered as he placed a row of milk bottles across the doorway.

We climbed the carpeted stairs and I heard Geordie locking the door behind us. It was a small room on the fourth landing. "Cosy, ain't it?" Annie commented with pride. It was bare except for an under-felt on the floor and curtains over the window. In a corner, stacked neatly, were a couple of bed-rolls and blankets. "Who do they belong to?" I asked.

"The other kids who come here." Geordie had joined us and was spreading his bed-roll out, so I followed suit in the opposite corner. "I shouldn't sleep there, Sal, that's where Ralph pisses when he comes in drunk. Jenny was lying there last night and he pissed all over her." I quickly moved myself to another corner. "Actually, we have all mod cons here. There's a lavatory next door, though no flushing water, I'm afraid."

"Why the devil doesn't Ralph use it then?"

"He's so drunk he doesn't know what he's doing; do you know, the other night he must have climbed over the railings to get in and missed his jump on to the window-sill, for we found him unconscious at the bottom of the base-

174

ment. I thought he was probably dead. Anyway, Annie and I lifted him up and put him in the room nearest the door. When he woke up next morning he didn't remember anything about it. Ralph's as tough as nails—he's a dirty-minded bastard, but you can't help liking him, can you?' Geordie summed him up in a nutshell. "Hey, wanna fag?"

"No thanks, I don't smoke."

"You a Christian and all that?" Annie asked.

"Yes—and all that!"

"Oh, God!" she groaned, and Geordie butted in:

"She's not like the others, Annie; Sally won't preach, she's not a religious fanatic—just a working Christian." I snuggled into my sleeping-bag. It was extraordinary, these kids all reacted the same if they discovered someone was a Christian. To them, a Christian was a religious fanatic who only had one topic of conversation—God—and someone who never smoked, drank or allowed his hair to grow. This was the idea which was put into their minds by naïve evangelists who worked amongst the beats to spread the Gospel; to these narrow-minded preachers, Christianity meant one couldn't go to a cinema or a dance, and they told the beats that juke boxes were part of the devil's work! These well-meaning people were doing more harm than good towards the daily practice of Christianity.

"She looks after the meths drinkers in the East End," Geordie was explaining to Annie. "I must come over and see them some time, Sal; perhaps I could help by conning food for you."

"Great!" I commented, as I took off my leather jerkin and made it into a pillow for my head. I was beautifully warm. The half moon was shining through the window, and outside the night was so clear I could see all the stars. Geordie and Annie lay enveloped in each other's arms in one sleeping-bag. I could see the burning tips of their cigarettes resting on the carpet. "Don't burn us to death," I whispered, and saw Geordie untwine his arm from Annie and put them out. I must have dropped off when I heard footsteps coming up the stairs; the door swung open and a voice said, "We're the police." Someone behind the figure that loomed in the doorway, giggled. "I arrest you in the name of the law," the voice came again.

Annie stirred. "I didn't know we had the London Palladium with us."

Three grotty bodies entered; in the dark with their long flowing hair, they all looked like girls.

"Who's here?" one asked.

I heard Geordie mumble, "F . . . off, we're trying to sleep."

"F . . . off yourself, you c . . ."

"Don't make so much bloody noise."

"Anyone got a fag?"

"Put the sleeping-bag down, Selby."

"Get off my back, man, I want a fag first."

"Shut up, you two, or I'll kick you in the . . ."

"I'm going to have a piss." He turned towards the corner.

"There's a lavatory next door," I suggested.

"You dirty pig, Les, do as the girl says."

"Who are you, anyway?" One of them was addressing me.

"I'm Sally," I answered.

"You're the Christian I met earlier this evening.'

"Am I?" I had not a clue to whom I was talking, and was too tired to really care. I wish they would all shut up so that I could go back to sleep.

"Selby, give us a draw?" The cigarette passed between them.

"God Almighty, I wish I were back in Chicago."

"Button up, man. This is one of the best derries in London."

"Man, I think it's crumby."

"Keep your bloody opinions to yourself, mate." It was Geordie.

"I wasn't talking to you."

"I was talking to you, though."

"Belt up all of you!" I raised my voice so as to be heard.

"F . . . off." One of them kicked me. I paid no heed.

"What's the bloody time?"

"One-thirty."

"Why can't you come in at a decent hour?" Geordie was talking.

"Because this c . . . here took us walking round looking for the bloody place; we started off in a derry with some froggies, but they expected us to lie in their shit, f . . . froggies."

"Do pipe down!" I urged, and curled myself into a smaller target for Selby's boot; he caught me on the ankle, and I pulled my sleeping-bag over my head so that I did not have to listen to their language. Again, I dropped off and must have been asleep for some minutes when a beam of light fell on me. I froze still. The beam slid from my sleeping-bag over to the huddled forms of Annie and Geordie. Everyone else was still sleeping. I suddenly realised that the torch beam was coming through the window; this meant that someone must be on the roof of the building opposite. In the silence I heard quiet voices and then a shout, "There he goes!" I jumped out of my sleeping-bag and crawled over to the window and edged myself up. Geordie was quick to join me, and Selby was on my other side. "Is it the fuzz?" he whispered.

"Must be, they've just shone a light in here."

"Look!" Geordie exclaimed. "It's Jock!" A crouching figure was scurrying over the roof; in the moonlight we could see the frightened face of the young beat. As he mounted a drain-pipe, three figures appeared on the roof in pursuit. They must have seen Jock, because they ran across the roof like lightning. "Go on, Jock, hurry!" I heard Geordie whisper. "He'll never make it," Selby was saying. Jock was parallel with the second floor windows, skimming with experience down the pipe when the policemen reached the top of it; but from our position I could see a police car making towards us from down the end of the road.

"If he keeps his head and doubles back and goes down the drain-pipe at the back, he could lose them."

"Not a hope, them fuzz know all the tricks."

Jock had decided his best way was to get to the ground

and run for it. He must have seen the approaching police car, because he was literally falling down the pipe, trying to make up time; and then it happened. He had outspeeded his own capabilities, and instead of stopping and losing seconds to regain his balance, he lost his nerve. He seemed just to let go. As he fell, he let out a blood-curdling scream. He lay absolutely still in the road, the three policemen above stood motionless, and we crouched painfully with every muscle taut, terrified for Jock. The police car skidded to a halt and two plain clothes men stepped out and bent over Jock's body. "Do you think he's dead?" I gulped. "God, what a fall! Did you hear the crunch as he hit the road?"

"He must be dead," Selby said.

"Please, God, no." And I began to pray. At the end of it I heard everyone awake say, 'amen' From the Middlesex Hospital we heard the ambulance siren, and then it appeared streaking towards Jock's prostrate body. It was amazing that no one else in the street had heard the rumpus, for it was a residential area. Jock's body was placed on a stretcher, and with three policemen to accompany him, he was driven away.

"Phew! Poor bloody Jock."

"What the devil was he up to there anyway?"

"Casing the joint, probably."

"Could be another derry, and when he heard voices he lost his nerve and ran for it."

"Jock's too experienced to do that, surely?" I argued.

"Och! You can never tell with these Scotsmen."

"Watch it! Keep down; there are some policemen on the roof still." We ducked and crawled back to our sleeping-bags. "Pass us the fags, Les," Selby whispered. The beam of the torch shone through our window. We flattened ourselves against the wall. "Keep as still as you can," Geordie ordered. "Put that bloody fag out." We all sat motionless, hardly daring to breathe. "Did you lot shut the front door when you got in?"

"Yeah, but I heard some guys come up after us," Les replied.

"Well, if they didn't shut it, the fuzz'll be in here soon enough.'"

The flashing torches continued to throw a strong beam into our room, but the six of us had by now crawled under the window and the beam could only flash on to the opposite wall. We sat in a close bunch for half-an-hour in complete silence. I think we were all wondering how Jock was. Eventually it was Annie who broke it. "Can I have a fag, Geordie? It's all quiet now, they ain't around. If I don't have one soon, my nerves are going to bust."

"Wait and I'll have a look." Geordie knelt under the windowsill and cautiously raised his head and studied the road below, and the building across the way. He watched for five whole minutes before he gave the all-clear. "Okay, let's have the fags."

"That was a close shave; I feel sorry for Jock when he comes round."

"If he comes round," someone dismally replied.

We all sat there musing; I shut my eyes, which were watering with the cigarette smoke. And then we heard it. An almighty crash. Silence. And then the heavy steps of boots climbing the stairs.

"Cigarettes out," someone hissed. We followed the loud steps into every room. And then the boots were on the landing beneath us. He threw every door open wide with a crash, and seemed to tour every room until he was satisfied that no one was hiding in any corner, nook or cranny. The boots were climbing the last few steps. They clumped to a halt outside our door. We waited. With a forcible crack the boot landed on the door and it smashed open. I saw a pair of eyes searching the room. This is it, I thought, I'm going to be nicked; and for the first time in my life I had no excuse. The boots entered, and smashed against poor Les. I heard him swear under his breath.

"Well?" the voice belonging to the boots bellowed out. I could not think of anything to say. My first thoughts were that they would need more than one black maria to take us all away. "Well?" came the voice again, "What's the matter with you all?" I recognised that northern accent instantly.

"You fraud, Ralph," I broke out, relieved, and everyone simultaneously burst into hysterical giggles. "Those wretched hob-nail boots of yours sound just like those the police wear."

"I didn't think it could be Ralph, 'cause his step was so firm."

"I'm dead sober tonight, if that's what you mean," Ralph protested.

"Why did you have to look into every room before you got here?"

"I was looking for Jenny, she ain't been around since I gave her those love bites and socked her one last night."

Everyone re-lit their cigarettes and settled back to relax. Ralph began to clump around. "Where's my blanket?" he demanded. "Hey, you bastard, you're lying on it." He thumped Selby.

"So what, mate, I got here first."

"F ... off!" Ralph let rip with both feet. Selby's shadow buckled up and he began to whimper. Les rose to his feet, his fists clenched, and a fight was about to start. "For crying out loud, all of you, we've had the police here once tonight. You're asking for trouble if we have a free-for-all here," I pointed out in desperation. "Ralph, you can borrow my blanket if you like." Anything to avoid trouble.

"Come on, let's get some sleep around here," a voice said.

"Here you are, Ralph." I produced the blanket.

"What's the time?" another voice asked.

"Four o'clock," someone replied. Ralph spread the blanket over himself, having taken off his boots; the smell was atrocious. I laughed to myself as I remembered the first time I had slept in a derry, wondering whether I was safer keeping my boots on or taking them off! It was fantastic that a year had passed since those hard and lonely days. A whole year since I left the Simon Community! I saw it in my mind as clearly as yesterday. Yet so much had happened, and I had learned so much since then, that I would have thought the memory of it would be distant. Not in the least.

At last I fell asleep. I awoke when the sun was pouring through the window. I looked at my neighbours, huddled together for warmth; I counted nine heaps which I presumed were bodies lying under coats, blankets and dust sheets. I glanced at my watch; it read six-fifteen. It was time I departed, for I had promised to meet someone at seven. As quietly as I could, I rose and rolled up my sleeping-bag, leaving my blanket over Ralph. I picked my way between the bodies and through the front door. Crash! Milk bottles went flying and splintered all over the pavement. I cursed volubly and scuttled out of sight, quite certain I must have woken the entire district.

As I passed the Middlesex Hospital I popped into Casualty to enquire about Jock. The nurse was very informative, and told me that he was suffering from shock and had broken both ankles and injured his head.

I was glad he was alive.

CHAPTER THIRTEEN

I FELT no pain, no sickness, no fear, just numb. Quietly and deliberately I counted the minutes. Without panic, or wasting what little strength I had left. I waited for them to turn to seconds. Time was running out. Now people were rushing madly round me; an ambulance had been called—but it would arrive too late. Pleasant, almost Utopian recollections flooded in a mass of confusion before me. I think I laughed, but no one heard it. Blurred, frightened faces, outstretched arms, sweet comforting voices slowly dissolved as I felt myself being dragged down, away into the vacant distances. So this was death? A soundless voice emerged from the vacuum: "Of course, delinquency starts at home, not in the schools." I gave a mental reply: "True! but you must remember that in this affluent society, adolescents tend to have much weaker family ties, and consequently they should be compensated by a stronger sense of guidance and security in their school life. Let's face it, this recent rise in delinquency seems to have occurred in conditions of an equally rising materialistic welfare." The seconds were passing, and I was dying, and delinquency was rising. Oh hell! what does it all matter? I am no longer a part of it any more, I'm dead. I had made a final comforting recession.

I lay between the crisp white sheets, gazing at the bare clinical walls. "You awake, dear? Can you turn over on your side so I can give you this injection?" I heard the words but they had no meaning. "Nurse Gallay, will you help me turn this patient on her side?" I wanted to struggle, but the effort was too great. I felt the pin-prick, and as a wave of nausea swept over me, I suddenly realised I had been given a fix. Struck with panic, I fought to keep my eyes open and my faculties functioning. What bastard had hooked me? So I was a junkie now. What did it matter? I slept. Now someone was leaning over me. My eyes were sore and burning and my head ached. I focused on the white coat, and then on the tourniquet round my arm. The doctor was taking my blood pressure.

"How are you feeling now?" he asked, on seeing I was awake.

"Peculiar," I grunted.

"Not to worry; that's the adrenalin we've pumped into you. It'll wear off soon. You gave us quite a fright."

"Sorry," I muttered dispassionately.

"Another few minutes and you would have been dead," he added for good measure. "You mean to say you've never had a reaction to penicillin before?"

"No, never."

"Well, don't you ever look at it again; you're highly allergic to it, and the next time you won't last long enough for anyone to call an ambulance. We'll give you a disc when you leave here, and make sure you keep it on you." He turned away to tell the nurse to continue to take my blood pressure every hour. I felt utterly stupid and deflated. After all I had survived these past few years, what an undramatic way to die! Not stabbed, not raped, not struck down with some terrible disease I had picked up in the grotty haunts I frequented! Just allergic to a penicillin tablet which the doctor had prescribed for blood poisoning in my jaw. I felt a buffoon.

Like everything that had ever happened to me this enforced rest was not without a purpose. It gave me the time which at one stage or another every one needs—to review the past and plan out the future. I wondered how long I could remain morally and mentally unharmed if I stayed on the road. I endeavoured to analyse my motives for returning to this arduous existence. Putting these factors aside meanwhile, I had to consider the inevitable that had happened. I was in love and due to be married in the following month. Our intentions were to emigrate to Australia. As exciting as it was, it became a painful decision to carry out. He would have to leave his family to whom he was very close, and I would have to leave my work. Like most engaged couples, we had our doubts; we would have been adventuring forth in the true pioneering spirit, penniless, homeless and job-less. But all that was important was that we had each other. Yet God had different plans for us both. Fourteen days be-fore the wedding my fiancé called it off. I was left stranded, bitterly hurt, yet I understood his reasons perfectly. My first reaction was to return to the road directly and lose myself in other people's problems, but instead I sat on my emotions and allowed my judgement to rule me. What future had I continuing work at that level? Eventually I would weaken and be dragged down. One can stand alone for so long, but the break would come! I kept telling myself that God had made a community, to live as a community, to be com-munity builders, not to be alone. I suddenly realised I had yet to learn to work compatibly with other people, and that as long as I failed to communicate or blend in with ordinary normal people I would never mature. The axle of existence amongst my beatniks was my daily communion with them; why should it be any different for others?

I ditched my dosser clothes and went home. My days were spent ringing up the employment bureaux, or visiting the local welfare departments in search of work. I wrote up to various social organisations offering my services. I had interview after interview. No one wanted me. What use was I to them unqualified? They were not interested in my prac-tical experience: they really could not care a damn for what I had achieved over the last four years, because it was not down in black and white on paper. I would be a menace rather than a help, because I would act on instinct and not knowledge, they politely explained. Angry and disillu-sioned, I walked about London convincing myself that someone, somewhere was waiting for a person with my ex-perience—somewhere there must be a niche which I could fit into. Deflated by continuous rejections, I began to seek employment in other fields apart from social work. I tried the BBC, the newspapers; I answered box numbers in the personal column of *The Times*, but it was as if I was doomed not to land a job.

The tables were reversed—I had come from a field of work where I was important and needed to a level where I was a nobody and utterly unwanted. At this juncture it would have been easier to turn my back on society and return to where I knew I was welcomed and accepted. At the same time I knew that if I took that course, there would be no reprieve. In my heart, I was fully aware that my work at that level had come to an end, yet the forces of progress niggled me and I searched for a way to continue this vocational work. I had experienced youthful lawlessness and a deliberate cult of amorality; now had come the time to use this knowledge to the best advantage. Yet how could I, when no one wanted to listen? It was like reaching a cross-roads, and each lead I took ended in a cul-de-sac. Coming face to face with my inadequacies, and frustrated by other people's intolerance, I began to yearn for my old life on the road. At least I was doing something constructive there, even if it was a poor second best because I was unqualified!

It was in desperation that one morning I contacted a professional social worker about the possibilities of working in a youth club. Her reaction was similar to everyone else—undisciplined and untrained, I could be more trouble than good. My heart sank.

"Of course, your answer is to get yourself qualified," she said.

"Me?" I replied in horror. "No one will have me with only three 'O' levels."

"You're young and intelligent enough to acquire some more."

"But I haven't studied for six years."

"So what? Believe me if you want to continue doing social work, you have no alternative; anyone else will tell you the same."

"They have," I moaned. "My brain's too rusty to start getting exams."

"Nonsense! Just a bit of will-power and determination, and of course self-discipline which you won't like." I left her office knowing well that what she said was true—I had no alternative, but whether I had the self-discipline to settle down to a routine day of swotting at books was another question altogether.

I worked out a time-table, decided to take two 'O' levels and two 'A' levels, and then viewed the possible courses I could take if I passed them in six months' time. I discovered exactly what I wanted in a college at Birmingham, a two-year course on youth and adolescent work. This became my goal.

I went down to Soho and explained my plan to the kids; it was greeted with the same scorn and bisbelief as I had received from my family. "Gi' over, Sal, yer no' cut out to be a book worm," Creeping Jesus had said. "Wot's goin' to happen to us while yer gettin' all that crap into yer head?" "So you're swapping sides and becoming one of them." This summed up their attitude. I had become a traitor. I wondered if I should ever come back as a professional social worker; whether I would have to earn their acceptance or whether because of my newly enrolled status, I would always be unacceptable. I said a sad farewell and returned to my books.

The first few weeks were unbearable. Sightless, my eyes read the words of the history book in front of me; diagrams on the opposite pages miraculously transformed into pictures of the ramp. At night my dreams were of the derries I used to sleep in. It was like an addiction—I lived, smelt, breathed, 'the road'. I was drugged with it, I thought of nothing else, it was like being hooked; but unlike drugs my craving was purely a mental state and not a physical compulsion, so it was just a question of mind over matter. Hating every minute of it, I forced myself to the library every day where I sat and swotted. I had little encouragement; understandably my friends and family were sceptical. This made me all the more determined to prove them wrong. I kept to this routine during the day, but most nights I managed to visit the ramp and see the lads. I received a tremendous welcome every time, intermingled with just a few curses because I had not been bringing them breakfast recently. Of course I was always forgiven, and affectionately they pulled my leg about becoming a student. They were far more sympathetic to my plans than the young beats. In fact, they were pleased. "Good on yer, Sal," they repeated numerous times. "Don't forget us, though," they always added. How could I?

I had managed to get myself accepted for college and was due to go up in the autumn. I had four months to kill, so I combined visiting the ramp with studying in order to try and get my brain functioning full-time, rather than at brief moments when I had nothing else to think about. One of my visits was to Kelly, who was now living in a cellar down on a Stepney bomb-site. Just like the old days; it was night, and my pockets were crammed with cigarettes and candles for them. I jumped the low brick wall and diligently side-stepped the fallen chunks of masonry. Once in the dip, out of sight, I turned on my torch and entered the jet black caves. Some of the lads were already asleep, curled up under newspapers. In the far cave I found Kelly and Pat sharing a cigarette. Pat jumped to his feet and offered me his milk crate. I declined, and instead squatted next to the horizontal body of Kelly.

"How are the legs?" I asked him, lighting a candle so as not to waste the battery in my torch.

"Shockin', Sal; 'aven't been able to leave 'ere all day to go conning, they're so painful."

"Those heavy boots don't help," I pointed out. "Anyway, let's have a look at them. I've got some first-aid kit on me." I rolled up his trouser legs and tried to pull off his soleless riding boot. It was not only stiff with mud but far too tight round his calf.

"When did you last take these off?"

"When you last dressed my ulcers; some weeks ago, ain't it?"

"Wriggle your foot, here it comes." The boot slid over his heel, revealing a pussy blood-soaked bandage. The smell was overpowering.

"Coo! don't 'alf stink!" Pat had never known what the word tact meant! I unwound the filthy dressing in order to see the ulcerated leg. From his kneecap down to his ankle the flesh had been eaten away as if some animal had been feeding on it for the past few weeks. Horrified, I dressed it and calmly said, "Leave the boot off tonight and I'll take you to the hospital tomorrow. I think you ought to have it looked at."

"Yer not takin' me no place, Sal. I ain' goin' there. They don't take to me and I don't take to 'em."

"But it needs attention; can't you forget your differences this once?"

"Nope; yer go on dressing it for me and it'll turn." I wished I had his confidence. I left them the food and moved out into the night air. I shuddered to reflect how I used to pass nights in that squalid depraved cellar. Briskly I walked across a few acres of derelict land, thankful to be out in the open. I bounded across another wall and on to the road. Under some arches and into a narrow unlit side street with boarded-up warehouses on either side. Half-way down this street, wedged together for support, were two crumbling houses. I tried to kick the door open but it would not budge, so carefully I slipped through the smashed window. I took three steps to the right, five forward, and three back to the left—one night some dosser would break his leg falling down that hole! I heard no noise and wondered if they were here. I climbed the disintegrating staircase and as I did so the sweet sickly smell of meths hit me like a whirlwind. They were here! I edged the door open and saw six bodies saturated in methylated spirits strewn out like flattened sacking. None of them would be wanting to tell me their problems tonight! I found a space littered with rags and bottles which I shoved to one side and promptly laid myself out. I was very tired, having not been out on an all-night stint for some months; it was strange how quickly I had adjusted back to a relatively normal pattern of existence. Sleeping normal hours, eating proper meals, digesting normal conversation; it had been my world once, and I had rejected it for this. Had it been worthwhile? Oh yes, a hundred thousand times yes. Every second, every minute had been worthwhile. I had not just been a part of a social revolution, but had been grounded in a social culture that society, rather than trying to understand, had deliberately rejected. No, there was nothing to regret, and the more I thought about my future, the more certain I became that to return to society and work from that level was the right move. Very content with life, now at home in either environment, I drifted into sleep.

I was wide awake and it was still dark. The lads were snoring away. What had alerted me so suddenly? Perhaps the pungent smell of the wood fire? I lay back, ill at ease. No one stirred. I closed my eyes and took a deep breath. That's strange, I thought, there was no fire when I came in earlier. I opened my eyes wide and momentarily froze with fear. "God Almighty!" I screamed, jumping to my feet and in one leap reached the door. As I opened it, my worst fears were proved; flames were leaping up the stairs. I rushed back inside and leaned out of the window; it was a thirty foot drop and no drain-pipe. "Get up you lazy bastards," I screamed, simultaneously kicking them to consciousness. I knew this would anger them and consequently wake them up. "Come on you drunken swine!"

Neil was the first to gather his inebriated wits together.

"And wot in the neem of the devil's the matter wi' ye?"

"Fire! Take a man with you and get down those stairs before I throw you down!" I lifted him to his feet and dragged another muttering man up and shoved him into Neil's arms. "Get out!" I yelled, thrusting them on to the outside landing. I grabbed at the insalubrious bundle of humanity nearest the door and hoisted it towards the stairs. Neil and his bundle had disappeared through the flames, which were beginning to creep towards us. The heat was scorching, and the noise of the devouring flames fantastic. The bundle in my arms collapsed in a heap on the landing, so hoping that God was on his side, I rolled him down the stairs and, grasping another staggering body, followed suit.

Like a pair of bullets we exploded through the fire head over heels. Now the flames were behind us and we were sprawled across the poor unfortunate bundle I had sent down ahead. He was still oblivious to his surroundings. Coughing and spluttering, inhaling smoke, we pushed and pulled the bundle into the street.

"Och, Sal! Is anyone else in there?" Neil was asking.

I gulped before replying. "Yes. Get these lads away further down the street in case the building collapses and then find a telephone and ring the brigade. Hurry now!" I exhorted. "Hey, lend me that overcoat!" I grabbed it from him and ran a hundred yards down the road to where I could see a puddle. As I laid the coat in it and soaked it thoroughly, I remember thanking God for having let it rain. Then throwing it over my head, I galloped like a charging blinkered horse into the burning house.

To this day I do not know how I ascended those stairs of charcoal surrounded by walls alight with flames. It was a miracle. The heat and smoke choked me, and my hands burned agonisingly as I groped for support. I flung myself from the blazing landing into the room. The wizened face of Joe, emaciated, smiling drunkenly at me, appeared through the smoke. Lying beside him was the comparatively virile baby-faced Sandy. "Up!" was all I could wheeze. Joe shook his head sadly and pointed to the crabbed body beside him. "Come on," I choked, as I hauled Sandy across my shoulders. Again he shook his head and gesticulated that we should get a move on. What the hell was the matter with him? If he could get on his feet he could totter to the landing—if there was any landing now? Sandy was becoming heavy. I turned to see if Joe was coming. I made one last desperate appeal, "Please, Joe!" and as I leapt into the flames I heard a surprisingly sober voice cry out: "Sal, bury me in my boots will you?" The intense heat was like a red-hot iron branding its stamp on shrivelling flesh. Leeched to Sandy, I floundered forward. We somersaulted through the air, then quite suddenly re-established contact with the ground. It was black and smouldering, and as I crawled to my knees it was as if I had landed on the spine of a hedge-hog. Someone was lifting me up. I wondered whether Sandy had landed in one piece. And what of Joe? What had he asked me to do about his boots?

"Hey, put me down, I'm okay!" I ordered. "Joe's still in there."

"No kid, not any more." We watched the roof crinkle slowly and finally melt into the roaring flames. Joe was in there somewhere.

It was not till the next day, when I was narrating this story in full detail to the police, telling them how I had managed to re-enter the burning building in a sodden overcoat, that I was corrected. "You must be a bit confused. It hasn't rained for five days." I sat dumbfounded.

"You're sure it was a puddle?"

"Absolutely certain. I couldn't have gone back in there for Sandy otherwise," I explained.

"That's the young meths drinker isn't it?"

"Yes," and as an afterthought, "I left the old one in there to make his own way down, but he wouldn't come."

"That was Joe Sayers wasn't it? Oh well, I can probably tell you the answer to that. We found him at the bottom of the gents' toilets the other night, stone drunk. Well, we didn't want to nick him, and since he obviously had a broken ankle, we dropped him off at the hospital, and quite by chance the following morning one of the constables was doing some routine checking round there and the night sister coming off duty told him that Joe had hobbled off with one of his meth-drinking mates before they had a chance to attend to him. Suppose he knew he hadn't an earthly chance last night. He's no real loss, he never did anyone any good while he was alive."

I was weeping. "What's the matter with you, you got the rest of them out alive!"

"It's not that. You got Joe all wrong." There was no point explaining to this police officer the epitome of my cause; the Joes who demanded nothing, the Joes who never advertised their plight, were the people the world rejected, judged and condemned. To me Joe Sayers is a hero, but to the world he was a dirty foul meths drinker, and my one regret which will be for ever with me is that I was never able to carry out that last request. Whether I become a detached professional social worker or remain an immature do-gooder, too involved for my own good, only time will tell, but I thank God He has shown me the potency of love and tolerance.

And that puddle with no rain? Only God can explain.

ACKNOWLEDGMENTS

I would like to express my appreciation to those in charge of Waterloo Station waiting-room where, whilst 'on the road', I sat and typed this manuscript without being moved on!

I would also like to thank Paddy, the Dobbie, Vick and Gorham families, who kept their homes permanently open to me.

Photographs 1, 2, 3, 4, 5, are by Romano Cagnoni (Report); photograph 6, 7, by Christa Feiler.